GROUSE & WOODCOCK
A Gunner's Guide

Don L. Johnson

Published by

krause
publications

700 E. State Street • Iola, WI 54990-0001
Telephone: 715/445-2214

Please call or write for our free catalog of outdoor publications. Our toll-free number to place
an order or obtain a free catalog is 800-258-0929 or please use our regular business telephone
715-445-2214 for editorial comment
and further information.

Library of Congress Catalog Number: 95-77308
ISBN: 0-87341-346-6
Printed in the United States of America

Contents

Dedication..5

Foreword...6

Acknowledgments..8

Introduction 10

1 Meet the Drummer 14
    Grouse Keep You Guessing 14
    Drumbeats and Heartbeats 23

2 Habitats and Lifestyles 30
    Breeding and Nesting 30
    A Place to Live 34
    A Varied Menu 37
    Covers and Coverts 47
    Facts About Flushes 58
    What About Winter? 62
    Grassland Grouse 72

3 The Wonderful Woodcock 81
    The Sky Dancer 81
    The Flight 89
    Finding Woodcock 94
    Scouting for Covers 98
    Away from the Alders 100
    Woodcock on the Run 105

4 Friends Afield 111
    Picking Partners 111
    It's Never Too Late 114
    The Old Professor 118

5 Thoughts on Dogs 125
    The Dogless Hunter 125
    Are Good Dogs Rare? 129
    Take Your Pick 138
    Canine Compatibility 142
    Beepers and Bells 145
    Canine Care 149
    Skunks and Porkies 155
    Traveling with Dogs 158

6 Guns and Gunning **161**

    Good Guns 161

    Better Guns 167

    Makings of a Wingshot 175

    A Fitting Gun 178

    Poking and Swinging 180

    The Lowdown on Loads 184

    Chokes and Spreaders 188

7 Odds and Ends **190**

    Maps and Backtrails 190

    Garb and Gear 196

    Road Hunting and Other Sins 203

    Game Care and Cookery 205

    Season's End 211

Appendix A   Suggested Readings **214**

Appendix B   Distribution of Ruffed Grouse
**   in North America** **215**

Appendix C   Ruffed Grouse Seasons in the United States
**   and Canada** **216**

Index **217**

For Lorraine, who for 45 years, has somehow managed to keep our house looking like a home instead of a hunting shack.

Foreword

It's a safe bet that most wildlife and sporting art is purchased not as an investment or because "it fits" a particular spot in a particular room. People, especially hunters, buy wildlife and sporting art because they look at a painting or a print and say, "I've been there. I know that place. I've felt that feeling."

The book you have in your hands is such a work of art. Having known Don Johnson for quite a few years as a writer, reporter, friend and mentor, I wouldn't have expected anything less. While it's crafted in a frame of information about grouse and woodcock solid as any hand-hewn border of oak or cherry, the main attraction is the beautiful word-painting itself.

Even if you've taken to the field only a time or two in pursuit of ruffed grouse or woodcock, you will seldom turn a page without thinking, "I've been here. I know this place." And just like a favorite painting, it will stir memories you'll want to take the time to savor.

Settling down to read the advance manuscript from one of my favorite writers was much like pulling a cherished birdgun from a well-worn case. The sense of anticipation was there. My pulse quickened. I anxiously awaited the sights, sounds, scents and tastes one only experiences in a lifetime spent in grouse woods and woodcock bogs.

I knew I'd be sharing the coverts with someone who has been there. And I knew I wanted Don to take me back there with him. I wasn't disappointed.

Grouse and woodcock hunters are notoriously tight-lipped about their favorite places to hunt. Don is no exception, but he's more than willing to share the glories of the days in those secreted shrines. He grants his readers the honor of sharing those times.

Page after page of fact and wit and wisdom pulled forth my own memories of grouse and woodcock hunting "back home." I can see vividly the expression on my dad's silver-stubbled face the first time he saw me flush and kill a grouse I could have shot on the ground. I can feel the pleasant weight in my hand of my springer's very first retrieve when he brought back a plump woodcock I was sure hadn't even been hit. I can smell the swamp water in my clothes on the afternoon I tried to cross a rickety, abandoned beaver dam to reach a tangled island I was sure held some unhunted birds (and it did, too).

On none of those occasions did I notice Don hiding behind a spruce tree or crouching behind a rock fence, but he must have been there taking notes, because now I find these memories here in this book. No, they're not necessarily in the words themselves, but they float temptingly like falling russet feathers between the lines. They are here in the places, the dogs' faces and the frosty October mornings Don so masterfully paints in subtle sentences and bright paragraphs.

After you've read *Grouse & Woodcock: A Gunner's Guide* I think you'll agree there's nothing left to be said except, "Don, thanks for taking us hunting with you." And as grouse hunters, we know there's no higher compliment.

Bill Miller
Executive Director
North American Hunting Club

Acknowledgments

Far too many have contributed to this book for me to recognize all of them here. The long list might well begin with Ernest Thompson Seton, the naturalist whose books I discovered in a public library as a boy. Following would be an ever-widening cast of characters—professors, biologists, foresters, dog trainers, shooting experts, photographers, and talented camp cooks among them. Most have been hunting partners. All have in some way enhanced my understanding and appreciation of the quarry and the quest.

Researchers and wildlife biologists who have generously shared time and expertise with me over the years have included John Kubisiak and Larry Gregg of the Wisconsin Department of Natural Resources, the late Professor Gordon Gullion of the University of Minnesota, Dr. Don Rusch of the University of Wisconsin, and Dan Dessecker of the Ruffed Grouse Society. If my conclusions differ from any of theirs, it is not because I do not respect their work. Different experiences often provide varied perspectives.

Through the pages of his *Grouse Tales* newsletter and personal communications, Ken Szabo has sometimes provided insights into ways of grouse and gunners in regions where I am not acquainted. That too, has helped keep me mindful that we all still have much to learn.

I am especially indebted to those editors who, early on, literally turned me loose to roam and write as I chose. During my years with *The Milwaukee Sentinel* they included Harvey Schwandner, Bob Wills, Harry Sonneborn, Trueman Farris and Keith Spore—each a hard-nosed newspaperman with a poet's soul.

My gratitude too, to other editors whose acceptance has allowed me to earn a living doing things I enjoy in places that I love. Glimpses of this book previously appeared in *Wisconsin Outdoor Journal, Wisconsin Sportsman, North American Hunter, Shotgun Sports, Wing & Shot, Gun Dog and Gun Digest,* as well as in *The Milwaukee Sentinel.*

Virtually all of the photos in this book were taken by me, but you'll also find a few that are the work of top professionals. Photographers George Cassidy, Ned Vespa and Sherman Gessert are valued hunting partners as well as expert shots with their cameras. I thank them for their help.

Kudos also to all at Krause Publications who took the results of my fumble-fingered struggles with a new word processor and rendered them into this book. I wanted my book to tell more than simply how, when and where to hunt. I wanted also to tell you why. It was Publisher Debbie Knauer who gave the go-ahead to that idea, Deborah Faupel, Book Acquisitions Editor, whose enthusiasm and hard work helped carry it forward, and Melissa Warden, copy editor, who made it all happen.

I trust that the reader will find that it was all worth the trouble. Good hunting!

Don L. Johnson

Introduction

It's one of those mint-scented mornings when bracken leaves sparkle with melting frost, when autumn fires smolder in the hardwoods, when an acorn's fall resounds in the silence...

The gun closes with the clean snick of parts worn to each other by long use. The spaniel whines softly, his stub vibrating until the tail wags the dog.

Remember now, how this dim logging road winds down through the sugarbush to that weedy clearing where a logging camp once stood? We'll hunt into that bit of breeze and the softening frost will hush our footfalls. Maybe this time we can take that old partridge at Mattoon's Camp by surprise. Maybe.

Then we'll poke through the alders, crossing and recrossing the creek to check on the local woodcock. Back then through the popples, and over to the Old Horse Barn covert, and...

But by then we'll just be setting our course by whims or wingbeats anyway.

"Let's hunt 'em up!"

The dog bounds away as if catapulted. Your heart leaps with him. It's grouse season once more!

* * * * * * *

To those so addicted, the magic of such moments is everlasting. Like Christmas dawn, when you were nine. That first bird rocketing through the fall foliage is as thrilling as the first Fourth of July fireworks you saw explode against the sky. The ruffed grouse, called partridge in much of its wide range, can affect one that way.

Exaggeration? Consider this:

At a state trapshooting tourney a while back, I was discussing fall hunting prospects with another grouse gunner.

"One flew across the road in front of me the other day. First one I've seen since last season," he related. "And look!" he added, extending a bare forearm. The day was hot, but he looked as though he had a chill. He had goose pimples.

"Grouse bumps. Just thinking about it!" he declared with a grin.

Put such a grouse hunter down within sight or scent of good cover and he is revealed as a breed apart. His sleeves are soon frayed and his pants will hang in fringes over scruffy boots. His coat will become torn, tattered by thorn, briar and brush.

Grouse dogs also begin looking thin and worn as the season progresses. A friend owned a setter whose tail was always wrapped in bandages after the first few days of the season. However, that didn't keep the dog's tail from whacking a swath through a thicket if the scent of grouse was there.

If you are already a grouse hunter, you will understand. If not, but think you'd like to be, I'll try to explain in the ensuing pages. Don't look here for magic methods for grouse hunting. Any book on the subject must leave much to learn. Rather, my hope is to introduce you to the best teacher—the bird itself. Just one smart old grouse can drive home the same lessons again and again. If there is anything upon which all grouse gunners agree, it is this: Old Ruff is, by a considerable margin, wingshooting's greatest challenge.

The true grouse hunter learns perseverance when boots are heavy and the game bag and shell pockets are light. The pursuit of grouse teaches humility when you think you've become a hotshot. And above all, it engenders love and respect for wild places and things.

What is it about the ruffed grouse that inspires such sentiments? Surely part of the answer is found in the times and places we seek him. The bird is quite a prize too; handsome and tasty.

However, we of the brushworn brotherhood (and yes, sisterhood!) are most attracted by the challenge. I suspect that we especially admire and revere the grouse because we simply are no match for him. Research has repeatedly shown that hunting has little influence on ruffed grouse populations in adequate habitats, although they may be vulnerable in relatively small, isolated covers. Grouse numbers do fluctuate, but the ups and downs occur in hunted and unhunted areas alike.

I also like the company grouse keep, particularly the woodcock found in many places I seek grouse during the first two months of the season. They seem an odd couple, but together offer majestic sport and a royal mixed bag.

Another great thing about grouse hunting is the length of the seasons. For example, in my home state of Wisconsin we start in mid-September. Foliage then is still so heavy that it's like hunting from inside a gunny sack. We do it though.

Then come autumn's blazes of color and dazzling Indian Summer days. Muffled drummings of cock grouse again challenge and mock from the hazy hills as the leaves swirl down.

Then, gray days in bleak, sometimes sodden creek bottoms. Winter's warnings in the wind. Grouse lying tight one day, spooky the next.

Then snow, and grouse whirring from conifers, or swooping from popple tops, or exploding from fluffy drifts, always with that uncanny timing that can leave you agape.

Good days, all of them. And, although the mercury may be shivering at the bottom of the thermometer, some of us will still be out there on the final day, paying the birds our last respects for the season.

That passion, that dedication, is what this book is really about. Mine are not intended to be the ultimate words on the subject of grouse and woodcock hunting. The truths, in fact, are many and varied. The ruffed grouse is a very adaptable and widely distributed species, native to a large range of environments. In habit and diet, it is quite a different bird in remote regions of the Rockies than in the Appalachians. Even in the Midwest, depending upon where we are, there are considerable differences in grouse behavior and hunting tactics. In Wisconsin, long ranked at or near the top in grouse production, we find the birds in big northern forests, in the hardwood hills, in the bluffs and coulees, in wooded river bottoms and in farm woodlots. In each of those habitats, the hunter must match the adaptations of the quarry.

If one's experience is limited to hunting in only one region, it is natural to adopt a quite provincial view of things. There is nothing really wrong with that. In fact, any time I am privileged to hunt with a local expert, I gladly listen to his well-earned opinions and defer to whatever tactics he has found to be successful. Moreover,

I am not surprised if eyebrows are raised when I mention some of my most fondly held opinions in such company. However, they are based on many thousands of encounters with the birds, and I can only say that they have served me well.

Included in this book are some beliefs for which I offer no proof other than anecdotal evidence collected during more than half a century of keen observation. I have been fortunate to have lived in or near prime habitats for ruffed grouse and woodcock most of my life, and also to have found a career that allowed me to travel widely, spending hundreds of days afield each year. Since those travels have taken me to the haunts of other species of grouse, from tundra to mountain to prairie, and because such pursuits are also of interest to most ruffed grouse hunters, I've also included some mention of those other birds.

I was not born to the traditions of grouse and woodcock gunning. As a boy, I knew no one who pursued the sport. Neither was I acquainted with any dogs with pedigrees, much less bird-pointing genes. Still, I knew early on that I would become a hunter of grouse. The realization grew as I paged through well-worn copies of sporting magazines that had been tossed out by a barber shop. At fifteen cents per copy, new issues of *Sports Afield*, *Outdoor Life* and *Field & Stream* were unaffordable, but the contents of the discarded ones were timeless. I could daydream myself into the covers painted by Lynn Bogue Hunt and follow Burton Spiller on strolls through the picturesque New England countryside. Although it did not then occur to me that the same pleasures could be found closer to home, I was certain that I would one day own a grouse gun and a grouse dog.

There is a wide range of thought on the ancestry and training of dogs, as well as choices of equipment for these endeavors. Having owned or hunted with virtually every kind of dog—and with no dog whatever—I hope to cast some rays of reason on the canine question. Further, after all these years of trying this and that, thither and yon, I want to offer some sound counsel on guns and loads, caps and coats, boots and gamebags. I hope you will find it useful.

So come along now. All through late summer's shortening days the spirits of bird dogs and hunters have been straining at their leashes, waiting for the magic words:

"Okay, let's go! Let's hunt 'em up!"

Don L. Johnson

1

Meet the Drummer

Grouse Keep You Guessing

In pictures, a ruffed grouse looks something like a pompous chicken with a fan-like tail and a pointy head. To the gunner, who usually calls the bird partridge, it often appears as gray-brown blur. Both views are accurate and also illustrate, in a way, something every grouse gunner should recognize. When it comes to hunting the species, it is hard to say anything with absolute certainty. A ruffed grouse encountered in the Canadian wilds is quite a different bird than one met in Wisconsin, and the bird found in Michigan coverts is, in significant ways, unlike its kin in the Alleghenies. So adaptable is the ruffed grouse, and so variable in its preferences, and even appearance to some extent, that it defies precise description.

I emphasize the point only because many of the facts told about ruffed grouse might be misleading. Observers who become intimately acquainted with the bird in a particular area may, quite naturally, tend to assume that their findings apply to grouse everywhere. They well may not.

No argument is intended here. I am appreciative of how much we have learned from professional wildlife researchers. As a hunter, however, I have always been most attentive to what I could learn from other hunters. If a man is acknowledged as the champion grouse-getter in his region, I don't care what he calls a grouse or what kind of gun he carries. I don't even mind if he

With its ruffs flared and its tail fanned, a cock grouse stands ready to intimidate a rival or invite a mate entering his bailiwick.

dribbles snoose juice in the cab of my truck. If he's willing to talk, I'm as intent as a bird dog with a nose full of scent. Over the years, I have been privileged with all kinds of people confiding in me their secret spots and private thoughts on partridges. If you are respectful and considerate, they will do as much for you.

Notwithstanding what I've just written, there are lots of things that all ruffed grouse have in common. One of them is the ruff of neck feathers that the bird can flare out like an Elizabethan collar. Both sexes have it. Another is the distinctive drum-roll sounds produced by the cock birds.

Although it often appears to be bigger and plumper, the average adult grouse seldom weighs more than a pound and a half. Its rounded wings, spanning about twenty-four inches, look stubby for the body. The most conspicuous feature, very evident in flight, is a broad, dark band near the edge of a large, fan-shaped tail.

Scores of color variations have been recorded. Hunters usually simply refer to gray and brown (or red) phases. Gray birds predominate in northern forests where conifers are common. Brown birds increasingly are the norm as one travels southward through deciduous forests. Protective coloration appears to be the most logical reason for the differences. Gray birds become almost invisible in the evergreens while those with rufous shadings blend better in the hardwoods—especially when the woods are littered with fallen foliage, and dead, brown leaves are still clinging stubbornly to oak limbs.

However, there is much overlap of color phases and there are many exceptions to the rule. For example, on a 1971 trip to the Rainy River district of Ontario, Hilman (Swede) Swenson and I noted a remarkable range of colors in the grouse we bagged. In one day's limit (five birds each), there were not only brown birds as well gray birds, but two of the gray birds had brown tail bands instead of the usual black. Tail bands of both black and brown were also noted among the brown birds. Adding to the variety, I also had shot a cock spruce grouse. All that along the same logging trails on the same day.

Virtually all of my grouse hunting has been done in the Great Lakes states. However, in Wisconsin, Minnesota and Michigan there is a wide range of habitats that approximate, to some extent, grouse haunts I have seen in Canada, New England, and even Alaska and Appalachia. As might be expected, we also see a wide range of grouse hues. Our northwoods birds are almost always gray, while those in the farm woodlots and forested hills farther south are usually brownish. In much of Wisconsin we see a mix ,

The woodpile was a comfortable backrest as the author took a break with Jim Mense and Chips after a rewarding morning hike along a northwoods trail in late October. (George R. Cassidy photo)

not only in the bag, but also on individual birds. There are gray grouse with shadings of brown and russet birds with hints of gray. We usually lump them as "intermediates." The individualism of the birds is evidenced by their plumage. No two are alike. For example, the barring on the tail feathers of each ruffed grouse is as distinctive as a fingerprint, and when a feather is plucked or molted it is replaced with another bearing exactly the same markings.

The colors of the ruff feathers and the tail band always match, but only the ruff feathers have an iridescent sheen. On black-banded birds, the flared collar shimmers with shades of greens and blues. On birds with chestnut bands, the ruff gleams like burnished bronze.

The grouse's sturdy beak—relatively short and slightly down-curved—tells of its varied diet. It is well-suited for snipping buds, snapping bugs, picking berries, and gathering greens. Like other members of the grouse family, its nostrils are hidden by feathers, a feature useful in winter. A look at the bird's legs and feet reveals several things too. The legs are well-feathered in winter to help keep them warm. The bird's feet become bigger in autumn too. Each toe then sprouts fleshy fringes, called "pectinations" by biologists and "snowshoes" by almost everybody else.

Some recent literature has suggested that the fringes aren't for hiking in snow at all, but are actually most useful for gripping slippery branches while feeding. I am not persuaded. Doubtless they sometimes help in the treetops, but I still believe that the primary purpose of those comb-like bristles—worn only through the winter—is to make it easier for grouse to walk in snow. They actually double the width of each toe.

Ruffed grouse do a lot of walking. The one exception is when snow is so deep and fluffy that hiking is difficult, even with snowshoes. (Having spent much time on snowshoes myself, I can relate to that.) At such times, the bird will fly between its roosting and feeding areas.

Although they have strong legs and sharp toenails, ruffed grouse don't scratch much for food. Somewhat surprisingly, their legs are not spurred. A fight between two male grouse may look as serious as a battle between gamecocks, but there is seldom any damage done except to the ego and libido of the loser.

Another prominent feature is a crest of spiky feathers, erected like a crown when the bird is alerted. Both sexes have crests, but those of the cock birds are longer. A hen's crest is shorter than one and one-half inches.

Its crest erect, an alerted ruffed grouse peers nervously into the woods around its drumming log.

Unless the bird is engaged in some obviously gender-related activity, such as drumming on a log or sitting on a nest, it is almost impossible to distinguish between cock and hen in the field. In general, the males are bigger, chunkier-looking birds with larger neck ruffs, longer tails and taller crests. However, while a particular bird may give the impression of being of one gender or the other, there is no way to be sure. Observations at drumming logs indicate that even the grouse sometimes have some trouble sorting out the sexes.

We can identify cocks and hens in the bag with some certainty however, without dissection. Since there is no single indicator that is 100 percent reliable, it is best to use a combination of known techniques.

For a long time, most of us regarded the tail band as the best signifier of sex. If the band described an unbroken arc along the edge of the tail, the bird was a male. If the band was indistinct in the middle, it was a female. Then we learned that a fair percentage of males also had broken tail bands, so we needed additional indicators. Here are the three simplest:

•There is a small patch of bare skin above the eye. You may have to push the skin upwards to expose it. If it is light salmon to bright orange, odds are heavy that the bird is a male. The same area is usually pale blue or grayish on hens, but it might be tinged with orange.

•Now take a look at the small feathers on the lower back, three inches or so above the tail. They are called covert or "rump" feathers. Pluck some out and you'll notice that they have whitish spots. Female grouse normally have only one of those dots per feather; males have two or three.

•Pull out the middle two tail feathers and measure their length, including the quills. If 5-7/8 inches or longer, it is an adult male. If 5-1/2 inches or shorter, it is a hen. Intermediate lengths may be either. (This method doesn't apply, of course, before the birds have attained full growth).

Although you'll get mixed signals from many birds, you can be pretty sure of the sex if any three of the above indicators point to one gender or the other.

Most hunters also are interested in knowing whether grouse they've bagged are mature birds or young of the year. Examination of the wings will tell. The outermost wing feathers are called primaries. Adult birds molt all of their primaries, a couple at a time, during the summer. Juvenile birds molt all except the two primaries at the leading edge of the wing. The newly-grown primaries of adult birds have smooth, curved tips. The same feathers on a young bird will have a less rounded, more worn appearance compared to their other primaries, which *have* been replaced.

Whatever their colors, the birds know how to make the most of them as camouflage. The patterns of the plumage form what is known as cryptic coloration. It befuddles the eye.

An immobile grouse, in cover of its choosing, can be virtually invisible. I often fail to see a grouse on the ground, even when it is sitting smack in front of my dog's quivering point. It usually is the same when a grouse is in a tree. It will perch there, stretched out to look like a stub on a branch, until the right psychological moment. Below, my dog is confused by the diffused scent spilling out of the tree. I recognize the signs, so I scan the tree tops. Nothing.

"C'mon," I tell the puzzled dog. "Bird gone. Hunt up another one."

"WHIRR-R-R-R-r-r-r!" goes the grouse. Behind me, of course. I twist around and shoot as it swoops, shoot again as it climbs, and then try to avoid the recriminations in the dog's eyes.

"Ding-donged bird! Just try that again!" I challenge. A grouse hunter is a glutton for embarrassment.

The bird's disappearing act never ceases to amaze me. While hunting along a hardwood ridge one recent deer season, I paused to lean against a big oak and watch the valley below. The woods were quiet, hushed by six inches of fresh, fluffy snow. About fifteen minutes into my vigil, I heard the soft fluttering of grouse wings. (Yes, when not departing in panic, ruffed grouse fly quietly.) Looking up, I saw a fine rufous bird alighting on a limb not more than twenty feet away. Seconds later, another arrived to perch in the same tree. Apparently they had been disturbed by another hunter and had selected that old red oak for a hideout. Even in late November, clusters of brown leaves were clinging stubbornly to the tree.

The grouse kept still. I suspected that, too late, they had noticed my blaze-orange presence and were reconsidering their choice of stops. My attention was diverted briefly by a deer appearing on the trail below. When I saw that it was a doe (I had only a buck tag) I looked back to check on the grouse. Gone! How could they be? I hadn't heard a thing. But then, as I stared at where they'd been, they materialized again. Even when I knew exactly where to look, those birds had tricked my eyes. No doubt about it: We walk by a lot of grouse when they're in trees.

I had a friend, long since passed on, who seemed to have X-ray eyes when it came to seeing grouse. Russ Mattison could see a grouse on a leaf-littered hillside one hundred yards away. He seemed able to spot where they were in snow roosts and he often spied them in trees. He worked for the old Wisconsin Conservation Department and for a few years was assigned to a grouse research project. However, no amount of exposure could have accounted for his amazing ability. I once asked him how he could possibly see the things he did.

"I just notice things that look like they don't belong," he answered. "With grouse, I see an upside-down 'V,' which is the head. I guess it just takes practice."

Well, I'm still practicing.

It isn't easy to get a clear look at a grouse on the wing either. Often we see little more than a fan-tailed blur, if the bird is glimpsed at all.

Considering time spent on the ground and time spent in the air, a ruffed grouse ought to have drumsticks the size of a turkey's and a breast the size of a dove's. However, survival depends upon those bulging breast muscles. Therein lies the explosive energy that blasts the bird upward and propels it to safety when danger is imminent. If the take-off reminds you of a rocket, the comparison is apt, for the sizzling escape flight of a grouse fizzles out quickly, often ending in cover not more than thirty yards away. If marked down and quickly reflushed, the bird will again fly with great vigor, and perhaps travel farther. However, if pursued persistently, it will be quite exhausted after three such flights.

Bob Dorney, while doing grouse research for the old Wisconsin Conservation Department during the 1950s, told me that if one could flush a grouse three times in rapid succession, it probably could be picked up by hand.

"They have low reserves of blood sugar," he explained. "What fuel they have is burned up in a few short, fiery bursts, and then they need time to replenish."

Keeping track of a grouse for three successive flushes is seldom possible in most covers I hunt, but I believe I have seen that theory borne out to some extent. On days when the birds are few and far between, and are flushing wild besides, I may try to follow up each flush. If successful in relocating the bird a couple of times, I approach its third landing zone with some expectation. Instead of running or flushing wild once more, it often will wait to be kicked out.

That the ruffed grouse is not a frequent or long-distance flyer is one of the reasons it is so revered as table fare. Because they needn't be supplied with blood for prolonged flights, those big breast muscles are as white as a domestic turkey's and much tastier. Grouse breasts are a gourmet's delight.

Although they often seem to outrun our shot, ruffed grouse will never set any speed records. One source reported clocking a grouse crossing an open area at fifty-one miles per hour, but that bird must have been in training for the Avian Olympics. A few seasons back, while Ned Vespa, George Cassidy and I were cruising leisurely down a northern Wisconsin forest road, we had a rare chance to pace a grouse. The bird winged out of the woods, banked sharply, and started flying alongside Ned's van at window level. We stayed even with it for as much as fifty yards—ample time to clock it accurately with the speedometer. Then, accelerating only slightly, the bird pulled away and veered back into the woods. Each of us agreed that it had appeared to be a grouse in a considerable hurry, and we all had seen a good many of those. Still, the speedometer had been registering only 31 miles per hour.

It is not blazing speed that makes the ruffed grouse hard to hit. Rather it is the explosive take-off, usually followed by some awesome aerobatics as it whirs away through a maze of trees. That big, fanned tail is its salvation. As the grouse tilts it this way and that, it can dodge, climb, dive and turn on a dime. More often than not, we can only wave a gun in salute.

Drumbeats and Heartbeats

The start of a new grouse year is marked on my calendar on that day when I first hear the reverberating announcement that Old Ruff is back on his drumming log. As those hollow thumps quicken, so do those of my heart. "Bup...bup...bup...bup...up...up-up-up-UP-UP-UP-UP-URRRRrrrrrrrr!"

It is a sound more felt than heard, and it reaches deep into the being of those who love the bird and the places it abides.

Drumming a welcome to another spring, a cock grouse mounts his favorite log and announces that it is time for the woods to awaken and the hunter's heart to quicken anew. (Wisconsin Department of Natural Resources photo)

It is said that grouse may drum any month of the year, but I have never heard it in midwinter in our latitudes. I do know, however, that a cock grouse will visit its drumming log frequently in winter. I have seen where, on a warm January day, he has practiced posing on his snow-covered perch, even trying a few wingbeats, his pinions leaving streaks in the snow.

It is in early April, before even the earliest shrubs leaf out, that drumming begins in earnest. The sound usually begins before dawn, before the first turkey gobbles, and continues on and off throughout the day. At the peak of the breeding season, which extends well into May, the grouse may be drumming out his challenge every few minutes, hour after hour. When really excited, he may wait hardly a minute before beginning another drum roll.

A smart grouse hunter will be taking some notes in early spring. Grouse scouting might be coupled with turkey hunting or early trout fishing. Both are activities that often occur in the heart of good grouse country. The sound of even one drummer is encouraging, and if you can hear two or more from one spot, autumn prospects are promising.

During years of abundance there may be four or five drummers per 100 acres of the best habitat. During lows in the population cycle, densities might be only one-fourth of that. But even if they slump far lower, a rebound is certain. The drumbeats are sounds of optimism and renewal.

If available, a grouse will always choose a large old log for its stage. Stumps, stones and other such elevations will do in a pinch, but drumming sites I've seen have nearly always been mossy trunks of fallen trees. An active site is easily identified, even if there is no grouse around, for there will be lots of the bird's distinctive droppings on and around the log. They are one to one and one-half inches long and about three-eighths of an inch in diameter. When the bird has been browsing on buds and such, they are uniformly brown and dry-looking. If the diet has turned to more succulent foods, the droppings are whitish in places. Recent, and probably active, roost areas are also revealed by such droppings.

Ideal drumming logs are located in spots that offer overhead screening, handy escape cover and proximity to food, while still giving the grouse a reasonably open view of all approaches. Such sites are usually in short supply, so there usually is a young male ready to move in should something befall the dominant cock of the woods.

A moss-covered trunk of a large, windfelled tree makes an inviting stage for spring drummers. This old oak has served as such for several years. The accumulation of droppings on and around the log shows frequent and recent use.

Bill Creed, a longtime research biologist for Wisconsin's DNR, documented more than twenty years of continuous use of one large log. He also reported that, after finding evidence that the resident drummer had been snatched from the log in April, 1988, he returned a few days later to find that another had already taken over the spot.

Predator kills at drumming logs are less common than might be supposed. Considering how boldly the cock bird announces his presence, one would think that he'd be easy pickings. However, he has a few things in his favor, including truly amazing hearing and excellent eyesight. Approaching a grouse undetected takes some doing. Even though the bird seems oblivious to all else during the few seconds it is drumming, it is supremely alert as soon as its wings are stilled.

There also is good reason to believe that at least some predators can't hear that dull, thudding sound. I got my first inkling of that many years ago. Walt Senn and I were sitting under an oak one moonlit October night, waiting for Old Cap to tell us he'd found a fresh 'coon track. The quiet was broken periodically by a grouse drumming to the moon, as they sometimes will in autumn. Then I saw a horned owl alight nearby.

I felt sure that the next time that grouse drummed, it would be sounding its death knell. However, it did drum again, and yet again, and when the owl departed it was flying in the other direction. It appeared that it had never heard the drumming bird.

I was met with skepticism when I mentioned the incident to a wildlife biologist. However, research has since shown that horned owls cannot, in fact, hear a drumming grouse. The owls can detect tiny rustlings and high-pitched squeaks at frequencies far beyond our capabilities, but the sound of a drumming grouse is below their range.

I suspect that some other predators may have trouble hearing drumming grouse. I've seen bird dogs react immediately to even the faintest cackling or crowing of a pheasant, but have never noted a similar response to the distant drumming of a grouse.

Years ago we lived at the edge of a woodland where grouse were common, and for two breeding seasons there, we had a drummer performing within seventy-five yards of the house. We could see him from our front door stoop before the gooseberries and honeysuckles leafed out. My Brittany spaniel knew all about that grouse. The drumming log was along the route of our morning walks. However, the dog was unable to see in that direction from his kennel, and he never gave any indication that he could hear the bird when it was sounding off.

It seems that quite a few people can't hear it either, although some just don't know what to listen for. It has a quality that is hard to describe. It is not caused by the bird's wings beating against its breast or the log, but is the sound of air "imploding" in the instants of vacuum caused by the flailing wings. It is sometimes hard to tell just which direction the sound is coming from, and it is always tricky to judge how distant it is. It has become a cliché to say that it sounds like an old tractor starting up, but it's true. Even grouse think so, and sometimes are attracted by a thumping engine.

Late one winter, a friend asked me to recommend a place where he and his two sons could take an early spring backpacking trip. The boys would be home from college for Easter vacation, he explained, and he wanted to spend some quality time with them in the great outdoors.

I recommended a southern stretch of the Appalachian Trail. That is pretty country anytime, and with luck, they'd even find redbuds and dogwoods in bloom.

Upon his return, I asked how the trip had gone.

"It was all right, but we were hoping for more of a wilderness experience. We never got away from civilization," he answered.

I was surprised because the trail runs through some regions that appear quite remote and wild. Had they encountered too many other hikers?

"No. It was just the sound of motors," he answered. "We'd hear them when we woke up in the morning. We'd hear them when we were cooking our supper. Sometimes we even heard them after dark."

I gave my best rendition of a drumming grouse.

"That's it! That's it! What *was* that?" he asked, beginning to scowl at my smile.

After I told him, he stalked off, muttering and shaking his head. I felt sorry about being amused. His wilderness experience had been spoiled by a sound that would have enhanced it greatly, if only it had been recognized for what it was.

Most hunters that hear a grouse drumming are inclined to investigate. The sound will at least lead you to an area where a grouse hangs out, and there's always a chance that you'll catch him unaware.

I have, on quite a few occasions, managed to get shots at grouse that beckoned me with their drum rolls. What usually happens is that they hop from the log when they sense the approach of man or dog, then run some distance before flying. Sometimes though, they will simply move to some nearby escape cover, perhaps a blowdown, and wait for the danger to pass. When that happens, they may flush within range or hold for a point.

If you are very careful or lucky, you might even come upon the bird while it is still on its log. I have read of such tactics being used to stalk the auerhaun, a big grouse living in the Black Forest of Germany. The trick is to advance only while the bird is going through its mating antics and hide while the bird is silent. Of course, it is not as simple as it sounds.

I did sneak up on a grouse that way when I was a youngster. I walked quietly until I judged that I was within one hundred yards of the sound (a deceptive thing to gauge). Then I waited until the bird began drumming. When it did, there was time for a few quick steps before he was silent again. I became familiar with the length of his drum rolls, so I was always behind another tree before he quit. It took patience. Five minutes of waiting, a few quick steps and wait again. He stopped for a while and I feared that he'd been spooked, but I waited a bit longer and he began again. At long last, I could see the blur of his wings through the brush, maybe twenty yards away. Since I had run out of trees to duck behind, I stepped into the open, my single shot 20 gauge cocked and ready.

The grouse was transfixed. We stared at each other, both indecisive about what to do next. I knew I had him dead to rights. It wouldn't hurt to let him fly a few feet, would it? Those guys in *Field & Stream* never ground-swatted grouse. The cock's crest was raised like a crown. Oh, he was the king of birds all right! My heart pounded as the blood lust of the young raced through my veins. My gun and my resolve were wavering. Who would know?

"BLAM!" The shot hurled the bird from its perch and it lay fluttering, breast down, in the dry leaves. Then a very strange thing happened. As I walked over to pick it up, the grouse began to drum, its wings beating against the forest floor in that same cadence I had memorized while plotting that bird's fate. It was eerie. The wings were stilled for only a moment before they began again, fainter now, as the bird drummed its epitaph in the rustling leaves. It seemed like an accusation. One more time the drum roll began, almost imperceptible, before the bird lay still at last. I don't know why. Perhaps a shot pellet had hit the drum button in the stricken bird's brain. What I do know is that it was a sad, sobering thing, and it had a profound effect on me. I never did that again.

2

Habitats and Lifestyles

Breeding and Nesting

Despite the ventriloquistic quality of its sound, other grouse seem to have no difficulty in homing in on a drumming cock. Visitors may be either male or female. Interloping males are usually sent on their way with a great deal of hissing and bluffing and a minimum of actual fighting. Surprisingly, a hen might get a similar reception at first. In time though, the boss bird becomes overwhelmed with her beauty and puts on a display that might be the envy of a turkey gobbler. Tail fanned, wings dragging, ruff extended, he struts and shakes his head, muttering sweet nothings until he has consummated the deal.

The hen has already prepared a rudimentary nest, usually a leaf-lined depression at the base of a large tree or stump. During the seventeen days or so that she is laying her clutch, she may revisit the drummer several times. Or, she may even consort with another within her hearing. Drummers will mate with more than one hen too. The sex ratio remains roughly equal from one year to the next, but there are usually quite a few non-breeding males, young birds who have failed to find good drumming sites and establish territories of their own.

Emerging from their eggs on a sunny day in May, these ruffed grouse chicks will soon be on their way. The nest has been built against the rotting remains of a big stump. (WI Department of Natural Resources photo)

After ten to twelve buffy eggs are in the nest, the hen incubates them non-stop, except for brief morning and afternoon trips for some quick bites of food. Leaves from a nearby aspen will do. With luck, she'll lead a downy little troop of grouselets away from the nest in twenty-three or twenty-four days. The chicks are ready to trot almost as soon as their down is dry and they can hop-fly to low branches when only a week old. A high-protein diet of insects is needed to sustain them during the first month or so. Then they begin switching to a varied diet of succulent greens, berries and flowers. The summer woods offer a veritable smorgasbord of grouse goodies. The chicks grow rapidly and by September they are hard to distinguish from the adults.

This book is not the place to discuss grouse population dynamics in any great detail, but some numbers may be of interest. Most research has shown that upwards of thirty percent of grouse eggs are destroyed by predators. Foxes, skunks, 'possums, raccoons and other mammals are the biggest nest raiders, but crows and snakes can be major offenders too. If she has been incubating less than two weeks, the hen will probably nest again, but her second clutch will be smaller.

Predators take a heavy toll of chicks as well, with hawks and owls beginning to play a larger role as the brood begins moving around. Others get lost from the hen, suffer injuries, or die from other natural causes. Of each one thousand chicks hatched, only four hundred are likely to remain alive in early autumn. The dispersal period in September is a particularly dangerous time. Their confused wanderings in strange territories make the birds especially vulnerable to predators. Predation takes a considerable toll in winter too, especially during years when scarcity of prey in Canada brings hungry goshawks south.

Of those 1,000 chicks, perhaps 180 will be around for their first breeding season, 80 will still be alive a year later, 33 will make it to their third spring, and 16 will survive to the fourth year. However, some smart old grouse beat the odds for quite a while. Of 1,300 grouse banded by Gordon Gullion's crews in studies around Cloquet, Minnesota, 3 lived to be 8 years old, and Wallace Grange, a pioneer grouse researcher in Wisconsin, recorded one that attained the age of 11.

Predation, parasites, diseases, and adverse weather all affect grouse to various degrees, and theories abound on what roles they may play in the roller-coaster ride that grouse populations take every ten years or so in much of their range. Two important things for the hunter to understand, however, are that (1) provided with ample good-quality habitat, the ruffed grouse can and will make a comeback after every low, and (2) ordinary hunter harvests seem to have no appreciable effect, overall, on year-to-year grouse numbers at any point in the cycle.

The cycle does not operate like clockwork, so long-term predictions are chancy. After the birds hit bottom, we usually see a few years of steady increase, a year or two at the top, and then a crash before it starts all over again. Grouse populations hit record lows in my region (in Wisconsin) in 1992-93. A marked recovery was apparent in 1994 and better gunning is anticipated for the remainder of the decade.

Here is evidence that eleven grouse chicks have gone to explore the world.

September is dispersal time for the young grouse. It is the time of the "crazy" flights when they sometimes fly into picture windows and land in city backyards. It once was widely thought that such birds were tipsy from eating fermented fruit. However, they simply have become confused in strange surroundings while looking for new homes. Mostly they make the move on foot, sensing that a flying grouse is a target for the ever-alert eyes of raptors. The male birds usually settle within a mile or two of where they were born. The hens travel much farther, so the fall shuffle minimizes inbreeding and fills vacancies that may have occurred in parts of the range.

Hunters may encounter "coveys" of grouse, especially early in the season. They may be broods that have not yet broken up—perhaps late hatches from a re-nesting. They also may simply be birds that have congregated at a particular place because of a favored source of food. Once they have left the brood, ruffed grouse are not gregarious birds, but they aren't anti-social either. Small groups of them often gather again in winter because each individual is drawn to the best available food and cover. The knowing hunter is drawn to those places as well.

A Place to Live

Ruffed grouse live virtually everywhere that aspens are found and some places where they are not. Their range extends into thirty-nine states and all Canadian provinces. The highest densities occur in the states bordering the Great Lakes and in their neighboring provinces, with Wisconsin, Minnesota and Michigan comprising the heart of the bird's range.

In the Great Lakes region, a typical spring density of drummers is about 3.6 per 100 acres in aspen-birch forests and 1 per 100 acres in the northern hardwoods, compared to 1.76 per 100 acres in hardwoods of the midwest, 1.6 per 100 acres in hardwoods of northeastern states, and only about 1 per 200 acres in the high forests of the southern Appalachians.

The differences are even more marked, however, when aspen forests are managed with grouse in mind. In Minnesota, intensive management of aspen trebled its carrying capacity for grouse. No other forest type has such potential for producing grouse.

On the other hand, the regions most dominated by aspen are also those most affected by dramatic ups and downs in the grouse population. Reasons for the fluctuations have been much studied and are not yet fully understood. The crashes are probably due to a combination of factors, including periodic increases in predation, adverse weather, parasitism and disease, none of which we can do much about. Mammalian nest raiders take a large toll, but birds of prey, especially goshawks and great horned owls, account for most of the predation losses.

We *can* do something about the habitat. High quality habitat will, to some extent, soften the bump at the bottom of a crash. More importantly, it sets the stage for a rebound, and the grouse will return if the habitat is there for them. It has always been so. Periodic disappearances of grouse have been noted on this continent as far back as the 18th century.

However, Dan Dessecker, habitat biologist for the Ruffed Grouse Society, has pointed to worrisome losses of the kinds of habitat needed by ruffed grouse and several other wildlife species. Young forests in various stages of growth are required, but data assembled by Dessecker shows that deciduous forests in the eastern states are maturing at an alarming rate. From Maine to Tennessee, acreage classified as hardwood seedling/sapling has declined by forty-one percent during the past twenty years.

In the Great Lakes region the problem is not so serious. Aspen forest types cover forty percent of Minnesota and twenty-two percent of both Michigan and Wisconsin. Moreover, commercial harvesting has increased dramatically in the past twenty years, creating much woodland in the successional stages. Those three states therefore offer the highest hopes for maintaining good grouse populations well into the future.

Nonetheless, since the late 1960s there has been a fifteen percent decline in the amount of aspen forest in the region. Principally, that is because private, non-commercial landowners control fifty-one percent (6.6 million acres) of the aspen in the region. Such owners are generally opposed to the clearcuts that would produce the desired regeneration. Therefore, their woodlands, by natural succession or conversion, are gradually being lost as prime wildlife habitat.

The way to create optimum habitat is to clearcut relatively small chunks of a woodland or forest on a rotational basis over a period of about forty years. That will provide ruffed grouse with cover meeting all of their needs, while also benefiting other species ranging from woodcock to white-tailed deer.

Open sunlight triggers rapid sprouting from the roots of felled aspens. The suckers may grow an inch per day and create stands almost as dense as the hair on a dog. Blackberries and shrubs prosper, and big bracken ferns may soon appear among the slashings. As they grow and create shade at their bases, the young aspens begin to thin out. In three or four years they are up to twelve feet tall and are ideal places for hen grouse to bring their broods. The overhead cover is excellent and bugs and other succulent food abound.

In eight to ten years, adult grouse begin making extensive use of such cutovers, and they continue to spend considerable time in them for another fifteen years while the trees grow ever taller and fewer in number. Drummers are usually located in stands less than twenty-six years old. Top densities of grouse will be found in aspen stands twelve to twenty-five years old, especially if associated with alders.

At age thirty-five to forty, aspens begin dying. If not cut, more shade-tolerant hardwoods will begin to take over. The resultant forest will carry few grouse.

While results will not be as dramatic, and grouse densities will never get as high, clearcuts of other forest types are beneficial too. Wherever they are found, ruffed grouse are keenly attuned to the variety and vitality of young woodlands.

Those who own woodlands and are interested in enhancing their value for wildlife can get much good advice and help from the Ruffed Grouse Society (451 McCormick Rd., Coraopolis, PA 15108). Those who do not own a woods can still play an important role by making their desires known and helping shape policies on the management of publicly-owned lands.

Every year, prime habitat is also being eliminated by changing land uses. During the past five decades I have seen countless coverts bulldozed away in the name of "development."

While I was the outdoor writer for the Milwaukee Sentinel, a reader wrote a scathing letter to my editor, criticizing a story I had written about woodcock hunting. "How could anybody slay those innocent little birds?," he wanted to know.

The irony was that the writer was a real estate developer, apparently oblivious that his business was a lot more injurious to woodcock than was mine. I have personally lost grouse and woodcock coverts by the score to subdivisions, shopping centers, resort complexes, golf courses and even airports. Since I have used some of those things too, I am not pointing a finger, but merely setting the record straight.

Hunters pursue their sport in accordance with rules designed to assure perpetuation of the species being hunted. Moreover, the hunter makes huge contributions through payment of special taxes on equipment; special fees for licenses, permits and stamps; and membership fees to groups like the Ruffed Grouse Society, Ducks Unlimited, etc. It is their money that supports habitat programs, wildlife research, game management and law enforcement. Oh yes, anti-hunters can point to some conservation programs that are supported by general tax revenues. However, they ignore that hunters are taxpayers too; they make their special contributions in addition to paying their regular taxes.

If you are chided for being a hunter, ask your inquisitors if they live in houses where there once were woods. Ask if they use the airport that replaced some fine cover for woodcock or cottontails. Ask if they shop at the mall where drum rolls of grouse were to be heard only a decade ago. Ask if they golf, and then point out that the water hazards are filled by a little creek that once meandered through haunts of timberdoodles. Then point out that, when hunters like you visited those former covers, the wildlife thrived, year after year.

Since we're not finding many grouse and woodcock in shopping centers and on golf courses these days, we can conclude that shopping carts and 7-irons are deadlier to those species than shotguns will ever be. Tell them that.

A Varied Menu

More than any other characteristic, it is the ruffed grouse's ability to thrive on a wide range of foods that has allowed it to adapt to such a wide and varied range of habitat on this continent. A complete menu of grouse fare might itself fill a book. A list of what it does *not* eat might be easier to compile. It eats buds, leaves, flowers and fruits from trees, shrubs and ground covers alike. It also snaps up virtually every kind of insect and a surprising number of other things. One grouse crop yielded a live salamander in a salad of watercress. Another contained a small snake.

Insects sustain the chicks during the first two weeks of their lives, but they soon are nipping at succulent leaves and berries. By late autumn they are beginning to sample buds as well, in preparation for winter when other foods are scarce. It is necessary for them to encourage the growth of bacteria that will enable them to utilize foods that, to us, would be as digestible as toothpicks.

It seems improbable that an adult grouse would ever starve. Chicks might become malnourished if a cold, wet spring inhibits insect production, but a grown bird has so many options that it's not likely to ever run out of provisions. Winter storms that sheath buds in ice are an occasional problem, but the grouse endure. Even though the bird stores little fat, it is capable of living a week or more without eating.

Knowing what grouse are apt to be eating—and when and where—is key to consistent success in finding them in fall. Some of the answers are obvious to anyone who is at all acquainted with the birds. They will consume virtually every kind of fruit and berry and a wide variety of greens, as long as they are available. Leaves of fern, strawberry, blackberry and clover are among their favorites, and jewelweed greens are a special treat until they are wilted by frosts.

Blackberries occur in many ruffed grouse habitats and their thickets attract the birds like magnets when the berries are ripening. However, grouse also hang around the briar patches at other times. The prickly canes help form secure havens for the birds and the leaves are among its favorite greens.

As the weather grows colder, they turn more to browsing on buds and catkins, but they continue to seek a varied diet. Leaves from winter-hardy plants are sought, along with any fruits that can be found, even after snowfall. Grapes, rose hips, holly berries and thornapples are savored, and of course, everyone knows that grouse hang around old apple trees wherever they can find them in overgrown surroundings.

There are some wet areas that I visit with expectation each autumn, for I know that I will find skunk cabbages there. The grouse know it too. They seem to have a passion for skunk cabbage, sprout, leaf and flower, and especially for that smelly plant's big, brown seeds.

I know too, where the waxy white fruits of poison sumac will draw grouse into a swamp just as the tamaracks' golden needles are sifting down. Those berries, and the identical ones borne on poison ivy, are especially rich in fat and the grouse love them. They also eat several other things that are toxic in one way or another to man and other mammals. In the Appalachians they feast on leaves of mountain laurel, a plant so poisonous that we are warned not to eat honey from bees that have been buzzing in the laurel tangles. No harm is done though, either to the bird or to the palatability of its flesh.

The ruby fruits of purple nightshade (named for the color of the blossom) are too bitter for mammalian tastes, but grouse like them.

Catkins, a type of bud found on members of the poplar and willow families, are important winter foods for ruffed grouse in much of their range. At a glance, most catkins look much alike, but not all are favored by grouse. The branches of this birch tree are full of catkins (top). A close-up shows a trio of them in detail. However, the alder's catkins (bottom right) are rarely taken by grouse. Their high tannin content makes them unpalatable.

There is a variety of dogwoods and they have a wide range. All of them bear fruits that are relished by ruffed grouse as well as many other birds. The gray dogwood (top) and redosier dogwood (bottom) are two of the shrub-sized members of the clan.

Availability of open water is not a factor in finding ruffed grouse. Although the birds may often be found in or near wet areas, it is the food and cover that attracts them there. Grouse usually get all of the moisture they need from their regular diets. They might supplement those sources with dew or snow. Some of the hill country I hunt is a long way (for a grouse) from any spring seeps or creeks. Yet, the birds thrive.

The dependence of ruffed grouse upon aspens during the winter has been emphasized many times, but other foods may serve just as well or better. Not all aspens are acceptable food sources. The flower buds of only certain mature, male trees are sought by grouse. Research has shown that the buds of those particular trees are the most nutritious. Others have higher levels of chemical compounds that affect their palatability, and even digestibility.

Those levels may also increase in the best trees at times. It has been suggested that it might happen when they are stressed by being overbrowsed by grouse. Whatever the reason, the bird's ability to metabolize the buds is inhibited. Other foods then may be very important.

It also has been found that the aspen buds are not nearly as nutritious in midwinter as they become in spring—another reason why grouse may go looking for other provisions. Many times I have seen grouse turning to hazel catkins, birch catkins, and seeds of staghorn sumac for at least part of their winter diet. Frozen grapes or other dried fruits are always savored, whenever found. As mentioned elsewhere, I've also found them favoring ironwood catkins over aspen buds, even when both were equally available. Noting such things will, in time, make one a more successful hunter.

Insects do not usually comprise a significant part of an adult grouse's diet, but when they do, the hunter should take heed. One season before the killing frosts, I shot a grouse that had its crop stuffed with grasshoppers. That suggested to me that his kin might be venturing a ways into an old stubble field, and they were. Slugs are often found in crops of grouse that have been feeding on autumn greens. Infestations of caterpillars can attract their attention too.

Opening weekend of 1961, Dave Duffey and I were hunting in the Hayward area, with the able assistance of Dave's little springer, Flirt. We were both about ten years into our outdoor writing careers then, and we figured that we knew how to find birds if anybody did. However, we were doing poorly. Late in the afternoon our bag consisted of only two woodcock.

Ruffed grouse may gorge on wild grapes wherever and whenever they can find them. They often return to feast on grapes long after they have been withered and frozen, and will even search under the snow for the fallen fruit.

We both were working for newspapers at the time (Dave was with the Milwaukee Sentinel and I was at the Eau Claire Leader-Telegram) and we each had a story to file. Nobody likes to write about getting skunked on grouse on opening day, so we kept looking.

I don't remember why we were hiking over an oak ridge, but when we did, a grouse whirred out of a tree. I managed to scratch it down and Flirt literally skipped with joy as she brought it back. There were other birds in those trees, but most of them flushed unseen behind the still-dense foliage. We did bag one other.

Opening the crop of that first bird, I found it squirming with some kind of caterpillars. I took one to a forester friend the next day. He identified it as a red-humped oak worm and told me they fed on oak leaves, and sometimes maples. He also told me where there were some local infestations of them. I parlayed that information into a couple of productive hunts before a sharp frost put an end to that bonanza.

Grouse have powerful gizzards that can handle tough seeds, but they usually aren't much interested in grains. In fact, there was a time when I would have told you that they don't eat corn. Years ago, the old Wisconsin Conservation Department tried to develop a pheasant that would nest in the woods instead of hayfields, where hens and nests often fell victims to early mowing. After they released a bunch of them in the woods of northern Dunn County, I was one of the volunteers carrying grain to some feeders that had been set up deep in the woods to help them through the first winter.

In the snow that winter, I saw tracks of virtually every woodland resident coming to the corn. Squirrels, rabbits, deer, jays, crows, and even foxes visited the feeders. But nary a grouse, although I often saw their tracks passing close by.

Wildlife researchers who were trying to trap grouse in New York back in the 1930s found that they had to dye corn red, orange and purple before the birds were interested in it. However, that apparently has changed, at least in some areas. To this day, I have never found more than a few kernels of corn in a grouse's crop, although I often hunt woods bounded by stubblefields strewn with waste corn. Reliable sources have assured me, however, that they have seen grouse crops stuffed with corn. Working the edges between woods and cornfields should therefore have special appeal for hunters today and in the future. Ruffed grouse do adapt, and I bless them for it.

There are several kinds of wild cherries, all of which are high on a ruffed grouse's grocery list when in season.

Bright red winterberries retain their color and their appeal to grouse long after most other wild fruits have been consumed or have succumbed to winter. A member of the holly family, winterberry is commonly found in lowland locations.

Large stands of mature, climax forest are poor places to look for grouse, but this is not due to any lack of foods there. Grouse relish many things found in the big woods, including acorns, wild cherry fruits and buds, birch leaves and catkins, maple buds and seeds, and ironwood catkins, to name just a few. It is the lack of good understory cover, not scarcity of foods, which makes the old woods so unpopular.

I could list literally hundreds of other foods found in grouse crops, but that might only confuse and overwhelm the novice hunter. One of the problems is that the kinds of available and favored foods vary so much from one region to another. Another difficulty is that we do not all talk the same language when referring to grouse goodies. Aspens are usually called "popples" in the north woods and "quakies" in the Rockies. The berry-bearing shrub that I usually call holly is a much different shrub than the holly found farther south. Winterberry and black alder are other names for our Wisconsin "holly." What I call hazelbrush is the shrub that bears hazelnuts (the wild kin of the filbert). Elsewhere in the grouse's range, the word hazel would probably refer to witch hazel, and so it goes.

Scientists avoid such confusion by using proper Latin names, which are the same anywhere a particular plant is found. However, other than priests and biologists, I am acquainted with very few hunters who know or want to memorize any Latin. I therefore have avoided it in this book.

The gist of all this then, is to encourage every hunter to make a list of favored grouse foods, not from any book but from his or her own field experiences. If you're lucky, you'll also be able to tap into the knowledge of someone who is familiar with the areas you wish to hunt. Old grouse hunters may be taciturn about the whereabouts of their coverts, but they seldom are secretive about their knowledge of the birds and their tactics for taking them.

Covers and Coverts

"How's the bird hunting?" asked the young man behind the counter as I was paying for the gas I'd just pumped into my pickup.

"Not too bad," I answered warily as I glanced out at my truck. There were no guns or other hunting gear visible. My dog, tired from two weeks of campaigning across northern Wisconsin, was asleep and out of sight in the cab. And as for me, I'd showered and

Highbush cranberry or viburnums are favorites on many grouse menus. Although the major range of this plant is south of the Great Lakes states, it has been successfully transplanted and appears to be thriving and spreading in some coverts farther north.

Both greens and seeds of jewelweed, found in moist sites, are savored by ruffed grouse. The plant is also called snapweed or "touch-me-not" because its seed pods, when mature, pop open explosively, scattering its seeds like birdshot.

shaved that morning and had even changed into casual clothes for the trip home. No brush pants. Not even a whistle lanyard around my neck. How did he know? He must have seen my puzzlement.

"I noticed your hands," he said, grinning as he handed me the change. I looked down. The backs of my hands *did* look as though someone had been playing tic-tac-toe on them with a jackknife. Then I noticed that he had a few nasty scratches too.

"Prickly ash?" I asked. He nodded. Then, for maybe ten minutes, we traded information on what the birds were up to, and where. We were, after all, blood brothers.

Everywhere I've traveled in this world, I've encountered some unfriendly kinds of vegetation, ranging from the clawing devil's club in Alaska to the stabbing wait-a-bit thorns of Africa. However, I'm convinced that none are more inhospitable than prickly ash. A dense stand of that tall, tack-sharp shrubbery can be just about impenetrable. Doubtless that's why grouse like to loaf in such places. And so do woodcock, where prickly ash occurs in river bottoms and other lowland settings. Knowing that has put a bunch of birds in my bag over the years.

A cock grouse surveys his domain from a log. His flanks are protected by a screen of prickly ash foliage in the background.

If prickly ash doesn't grow where you hunt, count your blessings, but get my point. Regardless of where you hunt, learning to recognize the right kind of cover will save you a lot of time looking for birds.

Covers and coverts are words often used interchangeably by grouse hunters, but there is a difference. By my definition, "cover" is a more general term applied to a particular complex of habitat. "Covert," on the other hand, denotes a smaller area, a special hideout; a hotspot for grouse or woodcock. The dictionary says that covert means "secret or concealed," and that is just how we like to keep our coverts. As to covers, most hunters will share their knowledge of them.

Because I know Wisconsin best, I'll use it as an example. There are about 123,000 square miles of ruffed grouse range in the state, including little farm woodlots and big chunks of federal, state, and county forestlands. There is a considerable diversity in vegetative cover and topography, ranging from beech woods and bogs bordering on Lake Michigan to the steep, oak-covered bluffs along the Mississippi River. There are dairy farms in the south, big woods to the north, and the flat central forests in the midst of it all.

From long experience, I can assure you that seeking grouse in the big north woods is quite different from hunting them in the coulees of the state's western counties. You change tactics again when your quest is in the central counties, and yet again in the agricultural regions farther south. The best I can do then, is to offer a few examples that would point a newcomer to the sport—or to the region— in the right direction. Only experience at ground zero can teach the finer points. Also, careful examination of the crop contents of every grouse will steadily build your store of knowledge of what grouse in that area are apt to be eating at a particular time of year. A grouse hunter has to become something of a botanist too.

The relatively flat, sandy, central counties present some classic examples of what grouse cover should look like—at least to me. It is the region where Aldo Leopold scribbled the notes for his *Sand County Almanac*, which, although not a grouse hunting book, contains some of the finest prose ever written about the sport. Much of the region is a mix of aspen and oak and pine, of shrubby marshes and alder-lined creeks, of clearings and berry patches, bordered with dogwoods and hazelbrush. Well, you get the idea. A lot of it looks "grousy." But of course, the grouse aren't everywhere.

I hunt there mostly along and near the creeks, not because grouse need the water but because the waterways usually are bordered by the kind of cover that attracts grouse, and woodcock

Large hawks and owls are said to account for more ruffed grouse, year-round, than all other predators combined (including man). Although goshawks are the grouse's most fearsome enemy—often making deep inroads during winters when a scarcity of prey drives them southward from Canada—other raptors, such as horned owls and redtails (above) are year-round threats in much of the ruffed grouse range. However, when provided with adequate habitat, grouse cope with all of their problems quite well.

too, when they're around. One shrub that always gets my attention anywhere it occurs is gray dogwood. It bears pearly white fruit in abundance, but the berries are often eaten up by the end of September. Another bush always worthy of note is the hazelnut, especially when loaded with catkins—slender, brown, scaly-looking buds that jut from the branches. Hazel catkins attract grouse as long as they are available, and that can be throughout the winter. But of course, those are only starting points. When scouting new territory, I like to follow the grouse I flush, even if they take me far off the course I meant to follow. They'll show you much about where they live, and why.

Recent slashings are worth a look almost anywhere in grouse range, and are magnets for the birds in the hill country I often

This spring-fed creek meandering through pines is in the heart of a covert often visited by the author. Beyond the conifers are oaks and birches, patches of aspen, and several openings edged with such grouse goodies as hazelnut, staghorn sumac, blackberry, bittersweet and grapevines. Such areas will hold grouse all seasons of the year.

Bob Mitchell and two springers, Squire and Chips, on a visit to the author's "Ace-In-The-Hole" covert. This spot reliably produced grouse and woodcock for nearly two decades before it was selectively logged.

hunt. Tangles of treetops left by loggers offer excellent escape cover, which the birds are quick to recognize. Especially attractive are south-facing slopes where oak has been selectively cut during the summer. Leaves cling to the felled limbs for a couple of winters, providing additional shelter from weather and predators. Hunt those sun-warmed slopes in winter and you'll find grouse tucked into the slashings like rabbits in brushpiles.

Yes, I do know that selective cutting of hardwoods is often bad news, while clearcuts produce young forests of sun-loving pioneer species that benefit grouse and other forest wildlife. However, there are exceptions to every rule. On south slopes, where the sun's rays are more direct, selective cutting usually lets in enough light to encourage reproduction, especially of oak, which is another species of high value to grouse and other wildlife. Also significant is that ironwoods are among the species thriving on the shadier sides of the same hills. Although long considered a weed tree by foresters, ironwoods are a valuable, and preferred food source for grouse. Even in areas where there were ample aspen buds available, I have taken grouse that had crops bulging with ironwood catkins.

Briar patches provide both food and cover for ruffed grouse. This bird was flushed from the blackberry tangle just behind the author.

A weary hunter and a tired setter head homeward after a late autumn day in a northern grouse woods.

When hunting steep country you should work the brushy draws, bottom to top. Stay ready for action all the way, but especially as you near the top. Dan Werner, an expert in hilltop tactics, also likes to hunt ridges by starting deep in the big woods and working out to the points. You'll get more open shots by working in that direction. If you have a partner, one of you should work along the sidehill, or perhaps along the bottom, while the other stays at or near the top. Grouse flushed from a slope will usually fly uphill, while those flushed near the top will often fly downhill. In any cover, two hunters will probably get four times as many shots as one hunting alone.

Hunting farm woodlots usually means working in and out of brushy borders between fields and woods. However, a woodlot that has some openings, and perhaps has been lightly pastured, will have other spots worth investigating. There may be a patch of blackberry brambles here, and a few clumps of hazelbrush there, creating pockets of cover much to a grouse's liking.

We used to hunt "stump pastures" a lot. I still do where I find them, but most farmers don't let their cattle graze in the woods any more. The ideal stump pasture is only lightly grazed, leaving brushy patches scattered throughout. It often has a stream meandering through it too. Dogwoods, hazel and blackberries are usually present, and so are grouse. Compared to most covers, hunting such places is like taking a stroll through a park.

You still can find such spots where traditional farming methods are practiced. It is necessary, of course, to get permission, and to be sure that the cattle are someplace else. Your dog may not chase cattle, but cows often chase strange dogs. Either way, any farmer will be displeased to see his herd galloping thither and yon with udders swinging wildly to and fro.

I have described northwoods hunting to some extent in my discussion of hunting without dogs and in other anecdotes, so you can glean some tips on that elsewhere in this book. Just pay particular attention to my mentions of conifers.

The value of evergreens in grouse habitat has been questioned because they provide hiding places for hawks and owls. I don't question that, for I have often flushed raptors from conifers when seeking grouse. On the other hand, I am hard put to recall any favorite grouse cover that has not had some conifers as an important component. There need not be a lot of them, for grouse will not venture deep into an evergreen stand. However, a few close-growing balsams, pines, spruces, cedars or hemlocks do make a difference. Grouse seldom are found in them in summer, but they often use them for roosting and escape cover during all other seasons. In absence of roosting snow, conifers offer the best protection from bitter winter weather. The heavy foliage not only stops the wind, but appreciably slows the loss of radiant heat.

A study in northern Wisconsin actually showed highest grouse densities in an area dominated by balsam fir, although aspen remained an important component. Alders were second best. Balsams have limbs extending to near ground level, a feature much appreciated by Old Ruff. On balance, conifers must be a definite plus or grouse would not gravitate to them. As with any wild things, the rules of survival are in their genes.

Facts About Flushes

Grouse and woodcock hunters record "flushes" much like muskie anglers count "follows." Any day that you have seen or heard a few birds, or have had a muskellunge so much as look at your lure, is a time worth remembering.

Flush rates will vary widely from season to season and region to region. There can be times and places when birds seem to be buzzing around you; other times when one can hike for many hours without a single flush. High times or low, those who are truly dedicated to the sport will keep at it, for the magic is still there. There is still the beauty of the landscape, the clean smell of the air, and the anticipation of what will happen at the next step—or the next.

Ken Szabo, chief drummer of the Loyal Order of Dedicated Grouse Hunters (LODGH), once asked his members to rank their grouse hunting outings in terms of flush rates. They rated seeing or hearing one-half bird or less per hour as "poor," one-half to one per hour as "fair," one to two flushes as "good," two to three as "very good," and over three as "excellent." Most gunners I know would agree with that assessment.

(Szabo's newsletter, by the way, is what I read first when I find it in the mailbox. Published bi-monthly, it is filled with interesting items about grouse and woodcock, research findings, new books, reports from members, and results of member surveys on hunting success, dog preferences, guns, et cetera. At $12 per calendar year, I consider Ken's "Grouse Tales" to be a bargain. The address is 17130 Chatfield, Cleveland, Ohio, 44111.)

Brighton and the author take a break and discuss strategy after a successful foray into one of their favorite coverts.

Whatever the rate, flushes are not evenly spaced throughout a day's jaunt. You may hunt high and low for hours with little success, then hit the jackpot. Szabo tells of a Wisconsin hunt in late October 1977, when he counted twenty-one grouse in one "flock" flush. That does not mean that all of the birds burst into the air at once, like a covey of quail. Ruffed grouse are more devious than that. Each takes flight on its own schedule, and the overall effect can be demoralizing.

Although I have never seen twenty-one grouse erupt from one place, it is not rare to find five or more together, especially early and late in the season. It usually happens something like this:

The dog is pointing in a latticework of old slashings. You vow that this time you are going to do everything right. You approach carefully from the side, so the dog can see you. Instead of staring into the cover, you try to keep your gaze about shoulder high, knowing that the bird will be up there before you can react. (It's a little like skeet shooting. You don't watch the hole where the clay bird comes out, you pick up the target a few feet from the house).

The dog's quivering tail tells you that there's danged-sure a grouse in there. You know how to read that dog, and if it were pointing a rabbit, its attitude would be subtly different. You swallow hard. A grouse has a heartbeat of 342 times per minute when at rest, but that is nothing compared to what your own ticker is doing at this moment.

"BrrrrRRROOOOOM!" A grouse angling left! **"BrrrrRRROOOOM!"** Another swerving right!...Stay with the first one!...Shoot!...Shoot again!...Oh no!...How could you miss a shot like that?

You lower the gun in disgust and start to reload. Adrenaline is still racing through your veins. You feel as if you've been standing at the epicenter of an earthquake. Then the after-shocks begin! One, two, three more birds blast from the tangle, each somehow timing its take- off to catch you off balance. Sometimes you feel lucky to fell even one bird from such a flurry of flushes.

Once in a great while, fortune smiles. A couple of seasons ago I got a rare double on the first two birds, a right and a left, as they flushed in unison. There were even witnesses. Usually though, the scenario is more like the one first described.

Most surveys I've seen indicate that gunners get shots at only a third of the grouse they flush and commonly bag about a third of those they shoot at. In other words, you might expect to get one bird

Brighton on point in snowy woods

for every nine or ten you put up. It is a real expert who can fairly consistently take two grouse with five shots. I once saw Ed Scherer kill five straight, but he is in skeet shooting's Hall of Fame. And even Ed isn't immune to slumps. I well remember him suffering through one while I was having a hot streak. Ed remembers too. I never let him forget it!

It takes a lot to discourage a real grouse hunter. A four-year survey in Pennsylvania, 1965-68, showed that they had averaged only 1.5 flushes per hour during that period. A sixteen-year study in New York showed hunters averaging only one grouse per three days of hunting, with each hunt averaging 5-3/4 hours. The New Yorkers bagged about one-fourth of the birds they shot at and lost about three cripples for every twenty birds they downed.

On the other hand, in the best years and in the best covers, it is not rare to have fifteen or more flushes per hour. I've had days when I flushed upwards of fifty grouse, especially during the highs of the early 1950s and again during the peak in the early 1970s. Undoubtedly, I could have flushed even more on some of those hunts, but you have to quit when you have a limit!

An imprint in the snow tells a story. A flying grouse was struck as it tried to dive away from a swooping hawk. It was snatched away just as it hit the snow.

My logbook also reveals that I shoot considerably better when grouse are numerous, although I wish it were the other way around. The reason is not that I get more practice when grouse are abundant. Rather, I think it is because it is so hard to stay alert when one tramps for hours without seeing or hearing a grouse. A flush now and then keeps you on your toes.

What About Winter?

Winter hunting for grouse is not widely popular, and that's all right with me. However, it has also been controversial, and that sometimes rankles. I have been told that winter hunting is "too easy," but not by anyone who has actually tried it. That opinion usually comes from someone who has hiked half a mile into the woods during the November deer season and, after an hour or so of remaining quiet on a stand, has seen three or four grouse stroll by.

"They get tame in winter," is the conclusion.

Predators hunt in winter too. Tracks and scat found near the remains revealed the killer of this grouse to be a red fox.

Patty comes back with a grouse that was flushed from the wooded gully behind her. Brush-choked ravines are places where grouse often hide from predators and frigid winter winds.

Brighton goes on point at the bottom of a south-facing slope during a December hunt. Here the direct rays of the sun have melted much of the snow and left bare patches. Such spots attract grouse, both because they are warmer during the day and because they provide better camouflage. Shadier parts of the woods are solidly covered with snow.

I try to tell such people that if they hiked that far and hunted that quietly in October, they'd see more grouse too. I'll also wager that if they were actually hunting grouse, those same birds would be flushing wild from the treetops or playing hide-and-seek in the evergreens. Such informants are usually unconvinced, but they aren't about to expend all that energy under wintry conditions to try to prove me wrong.

Others will tell you that shooting grouse in December and January is going to put serious dents in the spring breeding population. If I believed that were so, I would put away my grouse gun after the deer season. However, I have never seen any suggestion of it in my own observations, and have yet to see any studies with convincing findings in that regard.

The fact is that, in Wisconsin at least, only ten percent of the hunters are still chasing grouse during the winter months. That

Deep, fluffy snow like this is good news for northwoods grouse hunters. Adequate roosting snow is a major factor in good winter survival of ruffed grouse. This old cabin sits in one of the author's all-time favorite spots, but you'll look hard and long to find where it is!

Winter conditions present different challenges to grouse hunters. On snowshoes, the author heads down a northwoods trail to try his luck one more time before the season ends.

Tracks help wintertime gunners find the whereabouts of grouse. These tracks, made during a January thaw, led to a spot where the bird had fluttered into an oak to feast on bittersweet berries.

those hunters also account for about ten percent of the season harvest is testimony to their tenacity. Winter hunting is not easy.

To a large extent, the grouse I hunt in winter are birds that have had little or no hunting pressure earlier in the season. For example, I know of some hardwood islands in the midst of large swamps. Wearing hip boots, you can slog to them before freeze-up, but hardly anyone ever does. Usually I wait until the ice will hold me. By that time, there may be deep snow as well. If so, I go there on snowshoes. The snow hides thin ice, so sometimes I break through. The water isn't dangerously deep, just cold. Friends, the grouse I get that way don't come easily.

A couple of winters ago, I led Joe Knight to one of those hard-to-reach hideaways. Joe is the outdoor writer for the Eau Claire (Wisconsin) Leader-Telegram. Although the snow wasn't that deep, we had brought snowshoes to help carry us over the thin spots. That didn't work too well. There was ample ice to carry Joe's Brittany spaniel and my shorthair, but before long we both had taken a ducking or two. There is an added challenge to climbing back onto the ice when your snowshoes are sinking into black muck under two feet of water, but I managed. "He's still pretty agile for an old-timer," Joe wrote later. Grouse hunting keeps one that way.

Of course, wet feet in January is no reason to quit if you're a grouse hunter, so we pushed on to the islands, finding a few more soft spots along the way. We found tracks and the dogs smelled birds, but the grouse must have been watching mirthfully from the pines that day. We heard but one flush, and that was from a tree. I broke through once more on the way out. Easy hunting indeed!

Webs also come in handy for late season hunting in the big north woods, where Wisconsin's season currently ends on December 31. Shooting while aboard snowshoes adds a certain challenge to the sport—especially when a grouse bursts from a snow roost almost between your feet. Shooting the bird as it emerges from a geyser of snow would be relatively easy if it weren't for the fact that your mind is convinced that you've just stepped on a land mine.

Snow is a big help in one respect. Grouse tracks can tell you a lot about where the grouse have been, how many and how recently. They'll also lead you to and from roosting and feeding areas. It is possible to track down and flush grouse from the ground at times. If the tracks end somewhere in the hardwoods, scan the tops of likely-looking trees in that vicinity. The birds do most of their winter feeding in trees and are most likely somewhere in the upper third of the tops. Aspens, ironwoods and birches should get your attention, but they aren't the only possibilities. Last winter I

Ed Scherer and his Texas setter, Joe, congratulate each other on a bird bagged during a December snowfall in central Wisconsin. Falling snow often seems to make grouse nervous. That may be because swirling snowflakes confuse their vision and make them more susceptible to hawk attacks. Falling leaves on windy autumn days can have the same effect.

Habitats and Lifestyles   69

surprised two grouse that were high in an old oak festooned with bittersweet. The one I got had its crop about almost one-fourth full of the dried, orange- red fruit.

Ruffed grouse usually roost in conifers in cold weather, unless there is eight to ten inches of fluffy snow. Diving or burrowing, they will snuggle deep in a drift, sometimes tunneling for a few more feet before settling in. It is rarely colder than 20°F down there, even if it's -30°F outside. To escape a period of killing cold, a bird might stay there for days.

Sometimes a fox or other predator detects a bird in a snow roost, but the risk of that is outweighed by the energy-saving warmth a grouse finds there. Another hazard I have heard about is grouse being trapped under a crusted snow. I have never seen any evidence of that, and think it must be very uncommon.

In really bitter weather, a grouse may forego its breakfast, but conditions must be severe before it will skip supper. They feed late, stoking up as many calories as possible to carry them through a long, cold night, and usually do not go to roost, whether in trees or snow, until after dark. That is prime time for horned owls on the hunt, and they account for a good share of winter grouse losses.

Once tucked into a snow roost, a grouse may hold really tight. I recall a time when my dog was pointing at a hole in the snow. I stomped and shuffled, but nothing appeared. I finally kneeled down to scoop the hole bigger, intending to show the dog that there was nothing there. That's when a grouse blasted out from the end of its tunnel a few feet away, showering me with snow. The birds also spend a lot of time in and around conifers in winter, meaning that they are usually out of sight within a few wingbeats if you see them at all. Pay special attention to patches of evergreens if the ground beneath them is bare when there is snow cover everywhere else. The grouse know that they're much harder to see in those places, and they'll hang out there when not actively feeding.

Another tip: When temperatures plummet, the air is relatively warm close to open water. Discovering that, a grouse might choose to perch on a limb overhanging a spring-fed creek.

Then there are the grouse we find by clambering around in the hill country. We can pursue them there until January 31. We concentrate on southerly slopes where the snow isn't so deep. In fact, the direct rays of the winter sun can expose bare ground in such places while snow is piled knee-deep just over the hill. If you know just where to look, you may find grouse bunched in such spots, but you aren't going to shoot a lot of them. Not while you're standing with one foot about a yard higher than the other.

Dan Werner and Patty with a hard-earned grouse bagged in the hills in western Wisconsin in January.

Gunning for prairie grouse often means shooting at longer ranges. Here the author takes aim at a flock of wild-flushing Saskatchewan sharptails.

So are we killing too many grouse in winter? I'm convinced that the birds in any of the above-mentioned places are under-harvested, and my records of shots-per-bird would prove it! But it's still grouse hunting, so that's where I want to be.

Grassland Grouse

In my travels, I have taken opportunities to pot some spruce grouse, blue grouse and ptarmigans. For the novelty of it, I once hunted the blimp-sized sage grouse, too. However, of the ruffed grouse's assorted kin on this continent, sharptails—and to a lesser extent, prairie chickens—are of the most interest to sport hunters.

Spruce grouse may be encountered by ruffed grouse gunners in forests of Canada and neighboring states, but they are seldom abundant, nor do they usually offer much sport. They aren't called "fool hens" for nothing. They aren't bad eating though, and Minnesota hunters harvest quite a few. (Their estimated spruce grouse harvest in 1992-93 was 21,000, compared to 543,000 ruffed grouse and 20,000 sharptails.) In Minnesota and Michigan, spruce grouse are often found in jack pine forests. In Wisconsin, as in the northeastern states,

A cock spruce grouse is a handsome bird, but the species is not much sought for sport. Its usual tameness is probably because its haunts are not much visited by man. Ruffed grouse also were once regarded as stupid, and they still act that way sometimes in regions where they are seldom hunted.

George and Ned move in to flush a sharptail that Brighton has pinned down on a prairie in south-central North Dakota.

A long-barreled, tightly-choked 12 gauge SKB double was just the thing for taking spooky sharptails on a windy day on the prairies.

they usually hang out in soggy spruce swamps. The bird is protected in Wisconsin.

Sharptails and prairie chickens were still fairly common in parts of Wisconsin in the 1940s. They particularly thrived on abandoned farmlands in the central and north-central counties. Due to drastic habitat changes, the prairie chicken has long since retreated to a few areas especially managed for a protected, remnant population. There are populations in several other states too, but only in Kansas, Nebraska and South Dakota have they remained in appreciable numbers. Kansas has the most prairie chickens, but in recent times only Nebraska and South Dakota have had concurrent seasons on both prairie chickens and sharptails.

The sharptail's range, though much reduced, still extends roughly from Upper Michigan to the state of Washington, and from Nebraska to Alaska. It is adapted to harsh lands and climates. Like the ruffed grouse, it copes well with winter. Its legs are warmly feathered, it readily browses on buds of trees and shrubs, and it snuggles into snow roosts on bitter nights.

For me, the sharptail presents a challenge surpassed only by the ruffed grouse. True, there seldom are any obstacles for the birds to dodge behind, but the shooting is often at long range. Sometimes the young birds are approachable, and they may even hold well for pointing dogs early in the season, but you can never count on it. In fact, I have rarely found it so in many encounters in Wisconsin, the Dakotas, Montana, Manitoba and Saskatchewan. Sharptails are usually wary, and after flushing wild, will fly from sight, flapping, gliding and chuckling. It's the laugh that really gets to me: "Yuk-yuk-yuk! Yuk-yuk-yuk!"

I recommend a 12 gauge gun and stout loads of No. 6 or No. 5 shot. In a double gun, improved and modified chokes will serve most of the time. I'd stay with modified tubes in single-barreled guns until late in the season. Then full chokes are called for.

Sharptails usually feed in early morning and late afternoon, often flying long distances from roosting cover to grain fields. If a flock has been undisturbed for a while, such flights are quite predictable. Hide in some cover along their route and you'll almost certainly get some pass shooting, but it won't last long.

If there is no water near their roosting and resting cover, they will stop for a drink on their way back after feeding. Their midday hours are spent in dense cover, usually patches of shrubs or trees. On a recent trip to North Dakota, Ned Vespa, George Cassidy and I, with three pointing dogs, literally surrounded a patch of bullberry bushes one hot afternoon. That was one time we got some solid points and some fast and furious shooting at decent ranges.

Art Schroeder admires a pair of sharptails taken during a combination big game and bird hunt with the author in southeastern Montana.

A rare pair of birds in most bags these days. This sharptailed grouse and prairie chicken were taken in South Dakota. The sharptail is on the left.

On the Canadian prairies, where small islands of trees are called "bluffs," a common midday strategy is to hike from bluff to bluff, sending a hunter or two to the far side of the cover in hopes of intercepting the birds as they are driven out. Often though, the birds are so wild (or "hawky" as the Canadians say) that you'll see them flying from a distant bluff that you were only thinking about going to.

Where sharptail and ruffed grouse habitats overlap, you are advised to learn the difference because rules for taking the two species usually differ. The differences are quite obvious—the ruffed grouse with its prominent fanned tail; the sharptail with its pointed posterior.

Telling sharptails and prairie chickens apart is fairly easy too. Going away, the prairie chicken is a dark-brownish bird with a squarish tail; the sharptail looks grayer and its tail is pointed. Coming at you, the prairie chicken's breast shows prominent barring; the sharptail's breast is marked with small Vs and fades to near-white toward the belly. In hand, the prairie chicken is seen to have yellow legs while the sharptail has feathered legs and blackish feet.

Hunters unfamiliar with prairie fowl might also mistake a young hen pheasant for a sharptail where the ranges of the two species overlap. Again, the differences are learned readily. All except very young pheasants have much longer tails than the sharptail's. You should also notice that the grouse's tail is distinctly edged with white. And when you hear that chortling departure, there will be no doubt. The sharptails are the ones with the dirty laugh.

A cock prairie chicken struts his stuff for a female visitor to his spring booming ground.

Graeme Paxton, one of the author's hunting partners, with a beautiful pair of South Dakota prairie chickens.

3

The Wonderful Woodcock

The Sky Dancer

It begins on some raw March morning before daybreak: *"Zeemp...Zeemp...Zeemp...Zeemp..."*

The buzzing monotone doesn't sound much like a love song, but you have to consider the source. Those nasal notes announce the return of the woodcock, by all odds, the oddest of birds.

His nicknames reflect the amusement he invokes. Timberdoodle, mudbat, bogsucker, night peck, siphon snipe and hokumpoke are but a few. However, the woodcock shrugs them off and goes about his business like the little gentleman that he is. And at the moment, his business is romance.

For reasons obscure to anyone hearing them, the timberdoodle's calls have been referred to as "peents." An old departed friend, Dr. Joe Linduska, once offered a more accurate description. He likened the notes to belches from a flatulent frog.

However, the woodcock has more tunes in his repertoire. The peenting is immediately followed by a twittering sound. That is the song the wind sings in the bird's wings as he spirals steeply towards the now-fading stars. The sound becomes faint, then louder, then faint again. If you look up into the dimness of early

Vaulting upward on twittering wings, a woodcock waves a quick farewell before ducking behind the nearest tree limb.

dawn you may see the bird on its next approach. It is making wide circles, at what, for a woodcock, are dizzying heights and speeds. Its altitude is perhaps three hundred feet, its velocity possibly thirty-five miles per hour.

Then comes the most remarkable part of the performance. The bird hovers briefly, a rush of liquid chirps pouring from its throat. Then it pitches from the sky as if its engine has stopped, zig-zagging like a falling leaf while a continued stream of melodic chirps cascades earthward. Just when it seems it must crash into a grassy clearing, the bird pulls out of its tailspin and lands in the exact spot from which it had launched. The whole thing lasts about a minute.

The sky dancing is kept up until daylight and is resumed as dusk deepens at day's end. At first all is in vain, for male woodcock leave their southern wintering grounds as much as three weeks earlier than the hens. In their haste to stake out territories, they push hard against the edge of winter, often enduring snowstorms and bitter cold. One entry in my logbook notes that three woodcock flushed from a southern Wisconsin spring seep on February 15, 1990. That is about a month earlier than usual. Much of January and February were quite warm that year, but in Wisconsin you can bet on more winter, come March.

The hens apparently make the northward flight more quickly, for they seem to be present soon after the peenting begins. Usually a hen selects a nesting spot with some overhead cover not far from a male's singing grounds. Then she goes for a visit. Her arrival is greeted with great glee. The sky dancer bobs and struts, his stubby tail erected and showing its white-tipped underfeathers as he spreads it into a tiny fan. Mightily impressed, the hen accepts his advances, then returns to her nest and lays four buffy, brown-spotted eggs that are nearly the size of grouse eggs. Her mate continues to advertise as she incubates.

Some nesting is said to occur in every state and province within the bird's range, but most of the breeding occurs well north of the Mason-Dixon line. If the nest is not destroyed by a predator (about half of them are) the chicks will hatch in three weeks. Their oddities are evident at birth. They split their shells neatly in half, lengthwise, and enter the world as big beaks protruding from tiny, mottled balls of fluff.

Off-balanced by their bills, woodcock chicks often steady themselves by raising their wings. A couple of years ago, Dick Matthisen came upon a brood of tiny timberdoodles. While the hen

Four mottled eggs, almost as large as those laid by the much larger ruffed grouse, comprise the usual clutch for a woodcock hen.

These eggshells tell that four woodcock chicks were successfully hatched from this nest. A longitudinal split in the shell—most evident in shell at upper left— is evidence that it was broken by an exiting woodcock and not by a predator. Woodcock, which do a lot of things differently, are the only birds which open their eggs in that manner.

tried to lure him away with a broken-wing routine, the chicks stood at attention in front of Dick's shorthair pointer.

"They had their wings upraised like they were surrendering," Dick reported.

Steady or not, the chicks are ready to march as soon as they're dry. Soon they are feeding on insects, using their bills to poke and pry and turn over leaves. It doesn't take them long to learn how to use them as probes for earthworms, either. In two weeks they are flying a bit and at one month old they can fly strongly. The broods break up between six and eight weeks after hatching.

Mature males weigh about six ounces. The hens are one-fourth to one-third bigger. A hen weighing nearly ten ounces has been reported. Both sexes have builds resembling softballs and bills like knitting needles. However, while it may look clownish to some, the little elf of the alders is a perfect example of adaptation to an ecological niche. The bill is highly specialized for extracting worms from moist ground. The tip of the upper bill can be flexed open to grab a worm two inches or more beneath the surface. Nerve endings in the bill are thought to help the bird find worms by taste,

Female woodcock are larger than the males, but the difference is not always readily apparent. With a dollar bill (well-heeled hunters can use larger denominations) you can quickly identify the sex. The female's bill is longer than a dollar bill is wide.

Close-up of a pair of woodcock. The one on viewer's right is the larger female.

smell or vibration. Extraction of worms is also aided by a long, rough tongue.

A timberdoodle's ears aren't far from the base of its bill. It is supposed that their location helps the bird hear movements of worms. The bird's big eyes, located high and far back on the head, are another curiosity. They allow it to see above and behind while its bill is stuck in the ground. All told, despite quips about it appearing to be assembled from spare parts, the bird's design is a model of efficiency and its lifestyle is a remarkable adaptation from its shorebird ancestry.

No feature serves the bird more perfectly than its plumage. A woodcock in hand is seen as a thing of beauty. The basic colors are shades of brown and cinnamon with tasteful accents of gray and black. The breast is tan. The effect is one of elegance. On the ground, on the other hand, the woodcock is rarely seen at all. It becomes as one with the earth and with autumn.

Although so often associated with ruffed grouse, in habitats and in the minds of hunters, the two birds could hardly be more different. The woodcock is migratory and its flesh is dark. It also has a far lower birth rate than the grouse, but a considerably longer lifespan. If a woodcock reaches adulthood it has a life expectancy of nearly two years. A fair number reach the age of seven or more and one banded bird lived to be fourteen.

The bird's range does not extend much west of the Mississippi River Valley. There are two migration paths. One extends from western Ontario down to Louisiana. The other goes from southeastern Canada through the Eastern and Southeastern states and winds up in the Gulf states.

Until recent decades, wildlife managers were not concerned about the bird's low productivity. The species was regarded as underhunted in much of its range, and until the mid-1970s, it actually appeared that woodcock numbers were increasing along their Central flyway. However, a gradual decline has been apparent in recent decades. The reason is uncertain. Habitat losses are at least partly responsible, but the growing popularity of woodcock hunting may also be a factor. With that in mind, the daily bag limit has been cut from five birds to three along the Eastern flyway. Some hunters along the Central flyway, upon seeing fewer birds in their favorite coverts, have also started practicing voluntary restraint by restricting their daily or seasonal bags of the birds.

Based on 1993 reports from cooperating hunters, the U.S. Fish and Wildlife Service said that gunners in the Eastern range

A hen woodcock on her nest. Her camouflage is almost perfect, except for her gleaming eye.

averaged 1.9 woodcock per outing, with an average season bag of 7. In the Central range, hunters averaged 2.3 birds per day with a season average of 11.

Because they come under federal rules for migratory birds, woodcock may not be hunted with guns capable of holding more than three shells. However, a federal migratory bird stamp (commonly called "duck" stamp) is not required.

The Flight

Someday if I meditate long enough in the coverts. Someday if the Lord allows me enough seasons to wear out another wagonload of boots. Someday then, I hope to know just one thing for certain about woodcock.

The answer I seek is not how to hit a timberdoodle as it twists and turns through the alders. I recognize the laws of chance as irrevocable and have become resigned to the odds. Rather, my wish is that I could be able to predict and follow "the flight" that flutters across our state each autumn. Not all of the time, of course. Not everywhere. That would take away the delight of discovering a bonanza of birds in a barren-looking bit of bottomland between here and there on a grouse hunt.

If even once a year I could predict the furtive comings and goings of those little oddballs with certainty, it would do wonders for my equanimity, to say nothing of my ego. However, it seems that there are so many weather-related variables, and so many idiosyncrasies of the quarry, that nobody has found all of the answers.

That does not keep me from trying, however, or from telling you how to do likewise.

The woodcock we seek in the green jungles of mid-September are "locals," and, if you know where to look, you can find quite a few. However, it is when the migrants start arriving from the north that things can really get busy. There is a rapid buildup in some coverts, with new arrivals joining locals that are loathe to leave.

In Wisconsin, the peak usually occurs during the second and third weeks in October. In the central counties, I expect the arrival of a major flight about October 20. However, the birds do not always appear on schedule, and they don't always stop where expected. They arrive and leave by night. A covert will suddenly be

The author admires a pair of plump woodcock taken during the mid-October flight through Wisconsin.

filled with birds that may stay for days or weeks. They are gone just as suddenly.

In some regions, the migrants gravitate to spots that are not much used by the local birds, but that is not the case in most of the places I hunt. One must be careful then, lest we overharvest the birds that would be returning to that spot to nest. Studies have revealed that the local birds actually are the last to leave, so they are present before, during, and after the major flight has passed.

The flight is usually a leisurely thing with the birds moving southward in short stages. They flutter into our moist woodlands like leaves carried on the wind. They often drift from one place to another while lingering in our latitudes.

Upon finding a hot covert suddenly empty in midseason, ask yourself if there has been a windy night since your last visit there. If so, your birds may just have moved a ways downwind (usually east and south) and are waiting in another covert in that direction.

"They get an agitation to move, maybe ten or eleven at night, and they just drift downwind," Milo Mabee once told me, adding, "They're almost lighter than air, you know."

After the peak buildup, they usually trickle southward a little at a time, until one night the remaining birds receive a signal that

Milo Mabee during a sortie into one of his favorite woodcock coverts

winter is on the way. They'll make their usual evening feeding flight, storing up for the journey, although they are already well-larded with fat. Then they depart in small bunches, riding the wind before a cold front, usually flying no more than fifty feet from the ground. They are bound for climes where the earth does not turn to flint at winter's breath. However, it may be December before they settle down in Louisiana. If the winter is mild, many stay as far north as Arkansas. But whatever their destination, their departures leave our coverts oddly empty and still.

Some hunters hold the notion that flight birds are bigger than the locals. Not true. However, one old-timer told me about another difference that made some sense to me. He said that the migrants flush and fly differently from the locals.

The flight birds are those that fly erratically to an opening in the treetops, often presenting the classic woodcock shot, he said. The locals, he maintained, were those that tended to stay low, twisting and dodging through the tangled cover. They knew the territory, he explained, and the best escape routes were programmed in their little upside-down brains.

Although the regulations may give us longer, gunners in the Great Lakes states are lucky if they get more than six or seven

Close-up of woodcock in hand. "The Moment of Regret."

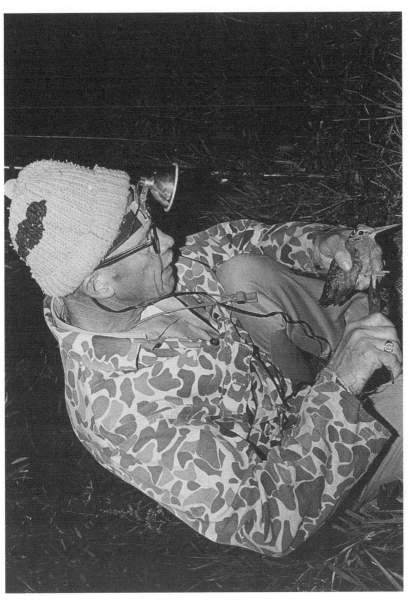

Harry Croy, who has devoted his retirement years and his northern Wisconsin farm to grouse and woodcock research and habitat development, bands a woodcock caught in a mist net on one of his fields.

weeks of good woodcock gunning. Only an exceptionally mild autumn will keep the birds with us until mid-November.

As they travel southward, woodcock are found less and less in the company of ruffed grouse. Where the grouse's range extends southward along the Appalachians, it is found at ever higher elevations, while the woodcock holds to the moist lowlands.

The timberdoodle would not be a difficult target if it flew in a straight line and stayed in the open, but its flight is extremely erratic. Rising abruptly on twittering wings, it twists and turns as it threads through the thickets. Then, at the moment you shoot, it will sideslip behind the biggest branch or tree in sight. Unless they are flushing wild, you'll get shots at most woodcock, but few gunners average better than one bird per four shots when working in thick cover.

Flushed timberdoodles seldom fly far, and can often be marked down again. However, watch for another trick. Occasionally, a bird will flutter steeply back to earth as if it has been hit. As you approach the spot, however, it takes to the air again. Unless you've seen the bird plummet earthward in a puff of feathers, keep your gun ready when approaching to pick up those "dead" birds.

The more years I seek those little brown birds, the more I love them.

Many years ago, I saw in the den of another hunter, a picture that made a lasting impression. It simply showed the head of a dog delivering a quail to the hand of a hunter, and it was entitled, "The Moment of Regret."

I think that every true hunter can relate to that sentiment. I feel it most poignantly each time I cradle a fresh-killed woodcock in my hand.

Finding Woodcock

Woodcock are literally where you find them. They are like will-o'-the-wisps, now here, now there, and then gone. Two covers may appear to have identical attributes to you or me, but one may hold woodcock year after year, the other one, never.

Now, you might think that anybody who eats squirmy worms would not have a very discriminating palate, but you could be wrong. Some folks say that woodcock can be pretty fussy about what they will eat. One earthworm looks much like another to you or me, but discerning scientists have identified subtle differences. (Well, maybe they aren't all so subtle. Even one who is not an earthworm epicure can distinguish between plain old garden variety worms and those that dwell under the manure pile.)

It does make one wonder though. Could it be only a matter of time until some wormologist (who is also a woodcock hunter) will come up with the answer to one of life's most enduring mysteries? Why will woodcock regularly gravitate to one patch of cover and ignore dozens of places that, to us, look just as inviting, if not more so?

If the answer lies in differences in worms, perhaps due to small variances in soils, you simply would have to identify your quarry's favorite fare, then determine the soil type where that species has its diggings. The dedicated woodcocker of the future might even carry a vest pocket soil testing kit and an annotated key to worm identification. The sport could then become as scientific as flyfishing for trout (another addiction to which grouse and woodcock gunners seem especially susceptible). However, until science digs deeper into such mysteries, we must go by what we see on the surface: field and forest, shrub and tree, hill and swale.

Other than actually seeing woodcock, the surest signs of their presence are their spidery tracks in muddy places, the holes bored by their probing bills, and the white splashes of their droppings. Call those "chalk marks" if you want to sound like a real timberdoodler.

In northern parts of the woodcock's range, classic coverts include alder swales and young woodlands (especially aspen) in early stages of forest succession. Some of the fastest gunning action I've ever experienced has occurred in clearcut areas where regenerating aspens were about as big around as broom handles and growing as thick as hair on a dog.

Not easy going, that. The slash left by the loggers has not yet rotted away and berry briars that flourished after the clearcut have not yet succumbed to the deepening shade. Oh yes, most flushes are unseen due to the dense foliage, for the aspens are just beginning to shed their golden leaves when the game is at its best. For added challenge, it's nearly impossible to swing a gun without whacking it against a tree.

Did someone say that doesn't sound like fun? Did I mention that it's not uncommon to have upwards of twenty flushes in an hour? I've had as many as sixty timberdoodles twitter from less than eighty acres of such cover.

Two veteran Wisconsin woodcock hunters, Jim Fisher and Bob Dreis, gave Jim's Brittany spaniel another sniff of the birds after a fine morning jaunt in west-central Wisconsin.

Some sorties into alder swales are just as memorable. Typically, tangles of alders follow the sprawling meanders of creeks, so figure on doing some wading. It will help too, if you practice shooting from various stances. Basic positions would be stooped over, kneeling, and straddling. However, endless variations will be discovered while ambling through alders.

There is an art to moving through alders. If you try to bulldoze through, they will grab you, pick your pockets and snatch your cap. So you learn to move deliberately, always thinking two or three steps ahead. That is, until the dog makes game!

I keenly recall a long-ago day when a spaniel sidekick and I literally wallowed into a swarm of woodcock along a little alder-lined creek in central Wisconsin. "Swarm" is the word that comes to mind because woodcock were buzzing around us like bees. In the confusion, it was hard to keep marks on fallen birds. With three down, I had to discipline myself to stop shooting until the dog had located them. Then, moving only a short distance, I shot two more. I regretted it almost immediately. I had parked the truck only about fifteen minutes earlier and bagging a limit had been too quick, too easy. But things do balance out. I well recall tripping through other alder tangles where my endurance was the only limit I reached.

While we're still in the alders, I'll mention something that might work for you somewhere, sometime. One of my all-time favorite woodcock coverts borders a half-mile or so of a northwoods creek. I was stumbling through the alders there one early autumn day, following the beckoning of the dog's bell and trying to get a look at the birds I heard twittering away. More often than not, when I did glimpse one, it was fluttering across the creek to alight where I couldn't follow. Woodcock aren't dumb. However, a light dawned after Chips, my woodcock-wise springer spaniel, had crossed and re-crossed that creek a dozen times. Having fished that creek for trout a few times, I knew that nearly all of it could be waded with hip boots.

The following day, wearing hip boots and a smug smile, I pocketed five woodcock by simply wading in the stream as the dog worked the cover on either side. Birds flying across the creek offered a high percentage of open shots.

I've used the same trick a number of times since, but it does have its limitations. Small creeks often are so overhung with branches and cluttered with windfalls that they are worse obstacle courses than the bordering brush. Other streams are too deep to wade. And of course, the strategy is only practical when hunting with a flushing dog. However, it *is* a way to enjoy relatively open and unimpeded shooting at woodcock in the creek bottoms.

How to find good coverts in the first place? I must tell you that blundering into that "bee swarm" bonanza was mostly luck. If I had stopped a quarter-mile upstream or down from that spot, I almost certainly would not have hit such a concentration of birds. I did make the most of that fortuitous find, revisiting the place often during the next several years. I never again produced such a flurry of flushes, but that spot almost invariably held more woodcock than similar-appearing stretches of that same creek. Doggoned if I know why. However, I am sure of this much: The availability of worms (of whatever flavor) is but one of many factors influencing the whereabouts of woodcock.

What's more, I'm glad we don't have all of the answers. If the woodcock's favorite coverts had some easily identifiable feature it would take much of the adventure from the quest, to say nothing of the added pressure it could put on the birds.

Scouting for Covers

Scouting new covers is one of the enjoyable things about being a 'doodler. There is the thrill of discovery and satisfaction of secrets held close to the heart. Serious woodcock hunters do not lightly share such knowledge, and when one does, it is with the expectation that the secret will still be kept sacrosanct from all others.

The finer points of finding timberdoodle coverts did not interest me that much during my first two decades as a grouse gunner. Like most hunters I knew, I simply regarded the timberdoodle as a bonus bird, a sporty little diversion found while poking around for grouse. There were days when I encountered quite a few, for ruffed grouse and woodcock coverts do often overlap. However, I didn't go out of my way to locate the little brown birds.

My attitude changed gradually. Acquaintance with truly dedicated woodcock hunters taught me that the birds were a challenge in their own right. I feel especially indebted to the late Milo Mabee. A barber in Neillsville, Wisconsin, Milo literally lived for the woodcock season. For decades, he chronicled the flights of timberdoodles in his central Wisconsin coverts, carefully noting temperatures, moon phases, direction and force of the wind, and anything else he felt might influence the comings and goings of the birds. So much did Milo revere woodcock that he had little time for grouse. He didn't really disapprove if you shot grouse while hunting with him, but he never let you forget that woodcock hunting was the business at hand. Milo always had good pointing dogs, but he knew woodcock ways so well that I sometimes thought he could show the dogs where the birds were instead of the other way around.

There was also something else that persuaded me to get serious about woodcock. When grouse were scarce, woodcock helped take up the slack. Once you've started to focus attention on them though, you're apt to find timberdoodles addictive. I began purposefully looking for woodcock haunts some thirty years ago, and my quest for good coverts continues unabated today. The most important thing I've learned is just this: You have to keep looking. You can never have too many places.

Scouting should not be restricted to autumn. In my ramblings throughout the year, I'm always noting spots that warrant inspection. You should poke around in such places in spring, remembering that woodcock are among the earliest migrants. If you flush a 'doodle or two from a particular popple patch or alder tangle, pay attention. Odds are good that, come fall, some southbound woodcock will stop in those same spots.

Listening for woodcock can also be productive in spring. Drive along a quiet back road as dusk nears. What you're looking for is an area that has grassy fields or openings near what you should already recognize as likely cover for woodcock. As the sun sets, stop, turn off the engine and listen.

I have already described the male woodcock's sky dance. Once you've heard that chirping song and those twittering wings you won't mistake them. If lucky, you may find a spot where you can hear four or more peenting males from the same location. It may end soon after dark, but I have also heard woodcock skydancing for hours. Usually that occurs on brightly moonlit nights, but there are exceptions. On March 25, 1985, I noted in my journal that a woodcock was still peenting at 10 p.m., despite an overcast sky and near-freezing temperature. Another time, I heard a woodcock peenting at daybreak although the dawn was dense with fog.

Locating singing grounds pays off because the hens almost invariably nest and raise their broods not far from where they mate. The males tend to hang around there all summer too. Therefore, it is almost a sure bet that there will be some woodcock in those parts when the season opens and for some weeks thereafter. Unless burned out by excessive hunting, the local birds tend to stay around, even after flights from the north have moved through.

Of course, the above scouting technique presumes that you are doing your spring listening in a region where woodcock regularly breed. The birds may nest in any state within their migration routes, but the major breeding areas are in the northern parts of their range.

The remaining scouting method is the one that is most enjoyable, and it is applicable anywhere along the woodcock's flight plans. Identify some likely-looking spots for inspection each autumn, and resolve to spend some time in them when you know the 'doodles are in. The serious woodcock hunter should have a special spot to serve as an "indicator covert." It need not be large, but it should have a proven record of harboring woodcock when the flight is in. Ideally, it is close enough to home to be visited easily (perhaps before or after work). Check it often during the period when you'd expect woodcock to arrive. A sudden build-up of birds there is a sure signal that they'll also be in some other coverts in the same latitude.

It is tempting, when the flight is in, to spend all of your time in tried and true places. However, it is important to keep adding new coverts to your collection because (1) nobody has too many good ones, and (2) the old ones have a way of disappearing due to changes in land use, or natural forest growth and succession.

Away from the Alders

It will also be useful to know that woodcock are not always found in classic alder/aspen types of cover. They also may be in thickets of gray dogwood and willow, on slopes covered with scrub oak, in fallow fields rank with tall weeds, in bottomlands bristling with prickly ash, and beneath all kinds of conifers. The list of potentially productive cover types is, in fact, long and varied, and depends upon where and when you are looking.

Woodcock normally consume more than their own weights in worms every twenty-four hours. They are generally thought to have two major feeding periods, one beginning about dawn, the other starting about dusk. However, there is ample evidence that they also feed—sometimes heavily—in midday. As you'd expect,

A couple of Pennsylvanians, Leonard Reeves, standing, and Nick Sisley, after emerging from some prime woodcock cover in Upper Michigan.

most mealtimes are spent in moist areas where they can probe for worms. However, woodcock also relish all kinds of insects, and even feed on many weed and berry seeds, so drier areas are not to be ignored. That is especially true if moving water is no more than an easy flight away. Stagnant water is disdained.

Even when on a diet of worms, which are eighty-five percent water by weight, woodcock appear to need fresh water. Unlike most birds, they do not raise their heads to swallow water, but suck it up through their bills. They have also been seen washing their bills after probing. Readily available water then, should be considered a prime component for any covert. However, that doesn't mean that hunters have to get their feet wet. Finding the birds in unexpected places has taught me to look high, as well as low.

One fine October afternoon quite some years ago, Bob Wilson, Jim Mense and I stopped at a north country farm owned by Bob's uncle. Too old and tired to keep up the fight, the aging lumberjack/farmer was allowing his fields, wrested from the forest stump by stump, to be gradually taken over again by brush and trees. However, to a bird hunter's eyes, it was a pretty place indeed. Margins of hazelbrush separated the woods from weedgrown fields on Uncle Leo's back forty. Within the woods, a creek meandered through a broad tangle of alders. Anticipating imminent encounters with both grouse and woodcock, we were panting like our spaniels as we headed for the woods. But first we had to cross a field rank with goldenrod, all gone to feathery seed.

Scarcely fifty feet from the fence, one of our springers erupted from the waist-high weeds, a buzzing brown bombshell seemingly balanced on his nose. As it outdistanced the dog, we recognized the object as a woodcock, but we all were too dumbfounded to shoot. No matter. Woodcock began fluttering from the weeds like moths out of an old horse blanket. Two woodcock here, three woodcock there. Woodcock, woodcock everywhere!

It was ridiculously easy shooting, for the birds had to fly more than fifty yards to reach any kind of woody cover. The thing to do, under the circumstances, was to allow most of them to make it into the alders where they could be taken in a more sporting manner. Of course, that is just what we did. After that first flurry, our guns were empty anyway.

Why were those birds congregated in the goldenrods, especially when a classic woodcock cover was close by? We can only speculate. With their bellies full of worms, they may simply have regarded that sunlit field as a more pleasant place to loaf than in those dark, dank alders. Or maybe they were seeking seeds, spiders or sundry insects for dessert. Whatever the reason, I've since been inclined to give that kind of cover a kick when it is near some more traditional timberdoodle hideouts. Sometimes it pays off.

And what's this about coverts in the conifers? Not many midwestern hunters I know regard evergreens as prime woodcock cover. However, upland pine stands are among the timberdoodle's favorite hangouts in the bird's Louisiana wintering grounds. We should not be surprised then, to find them in similar covers elsewhere.

I've had some memorable encounters with woodcock amid pines, spruces and firs. Like the time Ed Scherer and I hit the jackpot in the jack pines. It was mid-October and we'd been scrambling and splashing through alder bottoms in north-central Wisconsin. After a two-hour trek had produced only two or three flushes, we decided to drive to a different area. The shortest route to the car took us over a ridge densely forested with jack pines. It was cover so unpromising that Ed's setter was walking at heel.

Beckoned by two dogs on point, T. J. Edwards advances into a tangle of cover to flush a woodcock or two.

However, not far into the pines, our heads were suddenly swiveled by the twittering of a woodcock's wings. We turned in time to glimpse a rotund, russet form disappearing into the greenery.

Joe, the setter, seemed frozen in surprise. Or was he on point? The forest floor was carpeted with brown pine needles and virtually devoid of undercover, but we could see no bird where the dog's nose told us to look. Nonetheless, a woodcock materialized when Ed moved forward. It zig-zagged for a ragged patch of sky almost directly overhead, and when Ed fired, it fell near the nose of the still-staunch dog. We were momentarily in awe, for Joe was not usually steady to wing and shot. We were even more amazed to see the bird take to the air again. Or so it seemed.

I recovered from my surprise in time to scratch it down, whereupon Joe proceeded to fetch not one, but both of the birds he'd been pointing. The second one had held so tightly that it was loathe to fly, even when its comrade had tumbled to the ground nearby. Woodcock are like that sometimes. We had at least a dozen more flushes in that patch during the next half hour. It proved to be the most productive place we found during a two-day hunt.

Another time, Dick Matthisen and I were exploring new covers in Michigan's Upper Peninsula. Our guide and host was Ed Erickson III, a newspaperman and kindred spirit in Iron River. Even with the expertise of Ed and his experienced setter, we were flushing few birds in traditional covers. A hard frost that week, followed by a cold rain, may have been to blame. However, after Ed steered us to mixed covers, including lots of conifers, we began finding fair numbers of woodcock as well as grouse. Almost all of them were huddled under balsam firs.

On the morning we were to leave for home, Dick and I decided to take a leg-stretching hike along the Paint River, near Ed's rustic log cabin. I was dogless at the time. Dick had his young German shorthair, Kirby.

Bounding ahead, Kirby headed uphill and began making game in a dense evergreen stand. We found him quivering on point under some pines. We closed in, expecting a grouse, but there was no bird there. Moving deliberately, Kirby relocated some fifty feet away, again pointing into the low-spreading limbs of young pines. I circled around to an opening, tensed for action, as Dick moved in for the flush. Watching for an airborne bird, I almost missed the flicker of movement on the ground. It was a woodcock, scurrying away from Dick and the dog as fast as its little legs could carry it. It flew when I whooped, but was gone before I could shoulder the gun.

That scenario was repeated, with variations, several times during the next hour. Kirby pointed and relocated again and again. We managed to flush seven or eight of those artful dodgers, but bagged not a one in all that greenery.

When you think about it, conifer covers have quite a bit to offer woodcock. Stands of evergreens offer two of the things woodcock look for: good overhead cover and a sparse understory so they can move about easily while feeling secure. On hot days, evergreens offer cool shade. Moist soils under the mats of needles are often good places to probe for worms. A variety of beetles and other insects can be found there too. Also, conifers provide yet another kind of cover that confounds gunners. But a bumbling bird with a tiny, upside-down brain couldn't figure that out, could it? It must be coincidence.

What all this boils down to is simply this: If woodcock aren't where you expect them to be, try looking where you think they aren't. It's surprising what can be learned that way.

Woodcock on the Run

Many readers might also be surprised at my mention of woodcock running from a pointing dog. They aren't supposed to do that. The timberdoodle's fabled tendency to hold tight is one of the things that endears it to hunters, and especially those who follow the pointing breeds. But don't count on it. Woodcock *will* run, and I think that they're doing so more each year. At least that is true in many of the places I encounter them.

I was in my mid-30s before I ever saw a woodcock running away from a pointer, and I could hardly believe my eyes. On that day more than thirty years ago, Milo Mabee's dog Gin was having a hard time pinning down birds in an alder swale. Time after time the rangy shorthair's bell fell silent, urging us to crash through the tangled cover, only to have the dog move off again. I was getting pretty tired of all those false points, but I knew better than to criticize Milo's dog.

"They're running today," Milo declared.

"Sure they are," I thought to myself as I wiped my brow. *"Woodcock are running through the swamp. Ha!"* The alibis a man will think up for his dog!

Brighton clears a hurdle while eagerly retrieving a woodcock. She's anxious to get the bird pocketed so she can go find another. Most bird dogs will hunt woodcock, but some refuse to fetch them.

We were some distance apart, the dog between us, when I heard the approach of the pointer's bell. I stopped and waited. A few more tinkles. Silence again. What was going on? The answer arrived shortly. A woodcock darted into view. It stopped, looking to and fro nervously. The dog's bell jingled again, closer now, and the woodcock sprinted by me, not fifteen feet away, its little legs a blur of motion.

I was still gaping when another woodcock appeared, running as swiftly as the first. A minute or two later, Milo's dog arrived. She paused to look at me in utter frustration. I told her that I owed her an apology. Then she was gone again. Jingle, stop. Jingle, stop. We didn't shoot many woodcock that day.

Woodcock will also take to the water to elude us. I haven't actually seen one swimming yet, but I've seen them wade. Hunting in a partially flooded lowland woods one autumn, Dick Matthisen and I were finding woodcock on little hummocks and islands. Noticing that one of the dogs had picked up some scent and was headed my way, I stopped sloshing and waited. Before long, a woodcock appeared, stepping smartly through belly-deep water until it reached a little brushy island. Not too surprising, perhaps, considering its shorebird ancestry, but it did confuse the dog and offered yet more evidence that timberdoodles are pretty tricky.

Now don't think that my remarks about trotting timberdoodles are based on only a few observations. I have witnessed it many other times. In fact, in some kinds of cover these days—most notably in dense stands of gray dogwood or prickly ash—I expect at least half of our woodcock encounters to involve running birds. Nor should you suspect that this is due to the failings of a particular dog. I have seen those little rascals scamper from canines of every breed, temperament and pedigree.

If running birds are frustrating to a pointing dog, woodcock that hold fast in such cover are equally vexing to the gunner. Picture this: The dog's bell has stopped (or its beeper has started) in the middle of what surely must be the thickest thicket on Planet Earth. Branches snatch and claw at you as you shoulder your way in. In the urgency of the moment, you decide to come back and look for your cap and glasses later.

Ah, at last you spy your noble dog, standing statue-still in the very heart of that jungle. Your heart leaps with pride and thumps with expectation as you study the situation. To proceed to where the dog is pointing would be folly. There is no way you could mount a gun in such dense cover. However, only fifteen or twenty feet off to one side, there appears to be a bit of an opening. Uttering soft reassurances to the now-trembling dog, you sidle towards that spot. "Whoa-ahh...steady-y-y..."

Okay, now what? Ideally, you could command the dog to make the flush. However, mine won't do that. Odds are, your pointing dog won't either. "*I am a pointing dog of distinguished lineage,*" Brighton's actions (or rather, inactions) clearly say. "*As long as that bird ain't moving, neither am I!*"

Some hunters have found magic words to break that spell. I know one who just says "You get in there!" Another simply tells his dog to fetch. When I try that, however, Brighton replies, with visible exasperation, "*It ain't dead yet!*"

Under those circumstances, you are left with no alternative. You go in for the flush. You know you haven't a prayer of getting a shot. You just want that bird out of there so you can get on with the hunt. Remember always to lean far forward, using your weight to bulldoze though. Don't worry, the cover is usually too dense to allow you to fall to the ground. If you do lose balance backwards, you may have to do the limbo to get out.

There are times when you have to back up and take another track, even times when you must drop to your hands and knees or squirm on your belly, and all the while that little bug-eyed bird is sitting there, waiting mirthfully until you are literally beak to nose. Yes, woodcock will hold tight, all right. Especially when you don't want them to!

The solution to such problems should be obvious: Hunt such cover with flushing dogs, or always hunt with a partner. A close-working flushing dog is just dandy in the kinds of coverts just described. Woodcock won't do much running in front of a fast-trailing flusher, and they won't do much sitting either. While the dog works through the thick stuff, you often can skirt around the edges, giving you a fair chance to actually see and shoot at flushed birds.

Hunting with a partner or two also will greatly increase the percentage of birds bagged. I have already made that point pertaining to grouse gunning, but it is even more true in pursuit of woodcock. When the birds are sticking tight in the tangles, you just take turns kicking them out. Somebody's almost sure to get some shooting.

Still, for sundry reasons, I spend a lot of time alone in pursuit of woodcock. Some of my hunting pals are scornful of them. "Even our cat won't eat the things," one declares. As if his cat is an epicure! Would you eat cat food?

But mostly, woodcock are shunned because they are too much trouble when bigger and better things, like pheasants, are in season. Such sentiments get no arguments from me. I have lots of coverts literally to myself. As for woodcock palatability, I'll address that later, but I'm starting to salivate already.

Now, at risk of giving some purists the running fits, I'm going to mention one other strategy for dealing with problem birds. Gang up on 'em with both flushing and pointing dogs!

No, I don't recommend it for everyone. You really have to know the dogs, and the dogs should know each other. Some pointing dogs become basket cases if other dogs bust their points. Still, you might be surprised at how often a pointer and a flusher will work as a team.

Elsewhere in this book I tell of how Ed Scherer's old setter, Joe, and my springer spaniel, Chips, used to team up on grouse hunts. Now the boot is sometimes on the other foot. Many of my friends own springer spaniels while I have a shorthair, and we do hunt them together. Brighton is an independent hunter in such company, and seems undistracted by what the springers are up to. On the other hand, Jim Mense's dog, Boomer, quickly caught on to Brighton's *modus operandi*. Upon hearing Brighton's beeper, Boomer goes directly to the point and flushes the bird. That is just dandy in some of the woodcock coverts I've described.

Brighton doesn't seem to mind, and if the bird is a runner, or one of those sticking tight in impenetrable cover, Boomer's help is a boon. On the other hand, when her aid isn't welcome, I can keep Jim's dog from butting in simply by turning off Brighton's beeper. Boomer hasn't yet tumbled to the fact that an immobile dog, or a bell suddenly falling silent, also means that a pointer has found a bird.

A more conventional arrangement that I've seen used with success is to take both a retriever and a pointing dog into woodcock coverts. The retriever, which is kept at heel until a bird is down, has as important a role as the pointer. In fact, I consider a dog that finds and fetches downed woodcock to be of greater worth in the coverts than a fine bird finder that has nothing to do with the birds after they're shot.

In my experience, setters are often indifferent retrievers. However, most of them will, with some encouragement, reliably locate downed woodcock and "point dead." More than just a few dogs, of whatever breed, are reluctant to fetch woodcock. That is puzzling. If the woodcock's smell is so distasteful (as some suggest) why will some of those same dogs hunt for them so enthusiastically? One theory is that woodcock have loose feathers that a dog dislikes having shed in its mouth. I don't buy that either. I've seen some of those same dogs spit out a mess of grouse feathers after making a fetch, then go back after another one.

To deepen the mystery, I have often seen a dog baffled when trying to locate a downed woodcock, even though I had marked it perfectly and could walk over and pick it up myself. I once watched my old springer, Chips, repeatedly pass within a few feet of a fallen timberdoodle that I could see lying under the alders. Once he even stepped over it. This was a dog who had enthusiastically retrieved hundreds of woodcock, and he obviously was searching diligently for that one. What was going on?

I am convinced that a woodcock is somehow able to withhold its scent for a time. I think that the bird does so by clasping its feathers tightly to its body, and that it often does just that when it falls wounded. If it has became sufficiently air-washed in flight, it will then be extremely hard for a dog to locate.

In time, some scent will emanate from the bird, or, if it expires, the feathers relax and the scent spills out. Therefore, on the rare occasions when I give up the search, I'll endeavor to pass that way again a bit later in the day. More often than not, the dog will then come up with the bird.

Wounded woodcock will try other escape strategies. They might burrow under any available cover. Other times they will flutter and run when man or dog approach. But those that move after hitting the ground are usually fairly easy finds for a good retriever, as are those that fall dead.

I still don't know why some dogs love woodcock and others disdain them. However, the foregoing theory explains, at least to me, why some are so confounded hard to find when the dog is trying.

I conclude with emphasis that woodcock hunting should be done with a dog. Period. And a dog that will fetch (or at least find) downed 'doodles is essential unless you want to spend more time looking for dead birds than for live ones. A motionless woodcock, dead or alive, can be downright invisible.

When someone who hunts woodcock without a dog tells me that he rarely loses one, I am frankly skeptical. I can't help but remember how often my own dogs have returned with dead woodcock I didn't even think I had hit.

4

Friends Afield

Picking Partners

I hunt alone a lot. Partly, that's because I hunt virtually every day of the season and don't always have a friend available when I want to go. Then too, I really enjoy poking around by myself, moving at whatever pace I want. Most of my explorations for new coverts are done solo, and my discoveries often are the high points of the season. Those with less time to spare usually want to go to familiar and proven places, and that's fine too. Times spent with old friends in old haunts are to be treasured.

I suppose that most of us wind up with our regular hunting partners in the same haphazard way we learn how to shoot. Hit and miss. There really ought to be a better way, because finding a good hunting partner is important. More important, in fact, than having just the right gun or even the best dog. A day in the coverts with the wrong company can spell anything from aggravation to disaster. The problem is, you can't always tell what kind of a partner a person is going to be until you're afield together. Someone who appears to be a regular guy at work, or even at the gun club, may turn out to be a real yahoo in the thickets.

Over the years, I had mentally drawn up the specifications that a topnotch hunting partner would fill, but until I began to outline this book, I had never written them down. When I did, I saw that I had scribbled something more than a checklist for scoring hunting partners. It summed up what I believe are the ethics and etiquette of our sport. I've boiled them down to eleven simple rules. See if you agree:

ALWAYS, ALWAYS practice safe gun handling and insist upon anyone you hunt with to do the same. The first reminder can be a bit casual, if to the point:

"I thought you were using a 20 gauge."

"I am."

"Oh, I thought it looked more like a 12 when I was looking down the muzzle a minute ago."

Anyone can have a lapse, but a person who has to be chided more than once about such carelessness should be avoided in the future. Furthermore, I expect gunners to be muzzle-conscious in respect to dogs as well. If someone's gun is pointing at my dog, I'm inclined to take it personally.

ALWAYS KEEP the whereabouts of your hunting partner(s) foremost in mind. Blaze orange clothing is a big help and should be worn by all, but in heavy cover you should also keep tabs on each other with a word or two, or just a short hoot, at frequent intervals. Pass up any low shots if you're not absolutely sure. If a flushed bird heads towards your partner, a shout of "Coming your way!" will alert him of the bird's approach and also of your location.

DO NOT give commands to your partner's dog. There may be some exceptions to this, but if so, the dog's owner, not you, should state what they are. On the other hand, there is nothing wrong with saying something like "Good dog!" when your partner's pup does something right. Dogs and their owners both like to hear praise.

NEVER CRITICIZE your partner's dog. If the dog is doing badly, its owner is probably keenly aware of it and doesn't need to hear it from you. If, in fact, you believe that he really doesn't know that his dog has thoroughly masticated the bird it just retrieved, you might just hold up its bedraggled remains before pocketing it and say something like, "He really takes a grip on 'em, doesn't he?"

DON'T SHOOT rabbits, squirrels or the like while in the company of a bird dog. Of course, if the dog owner does it, it's okay, but most bird hunters don't want their dogs to be encouraged to hunt critters without feathers.

BE VIGILANT for signs of canine incompatibility. If you have a dog that is stealing another's points, busting birds, or otherwise hampering your partner's dog's performance, promptly apologize and take appropriate action. Expect anyone else to do the same if it is their dog bedeviling yours. Interactions between dogs are hard to figure. It is a competition-dominance thing and it is unpredictable. A dog that performs perfectly with most others can prove to be a real pain in the company of a particular partner. Remedy: Don't hunt them together. They may start working better together some day, but the middle of a long-anticipated hunt is not the time to let them work it out. Few things can ruin a hunt, or a friendship, faster than conflicts over dogs.

KEEP SECRET the whereabouts of any special coverts that another has shared with you in confidence. There are no words to describe one who betrays such a trust, although there are several (all unprintable) that come close.

AVOID SUSPICION of being a "claimer." That is a person who manages to get off a shot almost anytime a bird takes to the air, and then, when it falls, shouts "I gottim!" irrespective of who else fired. There certainly are times when two gunners shoot simultaneously at the same bird, and it may well be that your companion isn't aware that you fired. If that's the case, why not just say "Nice shot!" and get on with the hunt? On the other hand, if a "claimer" pattern becomes apparent, start hunting farther away from the offender. The next county should be far enough. Real claimers invariably have other serious deficiencies too.

TREAT THE QUARRY with the reverence and respect it deserves. Search diligently for all downed game and be sure that it is kept fit for the table.

ALWAYS HEED all game laws and "No Trespassing" signs. Hunting is supposed to be a pleasant pastime. Aside from the ethics of staying on the right side of laws and fences, why would anyone want to risk having the day spoiled by a grim-faced warden or an irate landowner?

DO YOUR SHARE, and then try to do more. If you have picked the right hunting partners, they will have the same philosophy and nobody will be overburdened. Some people like to drive, some like to cook, but whatever the chores—cleaning the cabin, splitting wood or doing dishes—doing your part will help keep a hunt a happy one.

That's pretty much it. You're free to add to the list if you like, but I think that the bottom line will still be the same. No slobs nor damn fools need apply. And when you think about it, the trick to finding and keeping good hunting partners is simply knowing how to *be* one.

It's Never Too Late

It was one of those mornings when luminous mist drifted down the south fork of the Flambeau River. It swirled through the rapids and rose in panting breaths below the falls. There were torch parades in the maples and aspens gleaming like gold in the rising sun.

Dick Matthisen and his German shorthair pointer, Mitzi, were waiting impatiently as I brewed coffee and mulled over plans for the day. There really was no hurry. After days of drenching rain, a cold front had dropped down from Canada, bringing a night that sparkled with stars and a dawn that glittered with frost. The grouse would have been moving out of the conifers as the sun glanced over the horizon. They would be heading for the trails to soak up some rays and pick some greens, then start ranging more widely for such goodies as thornapples, wintergreen berries and hazel catkins.

"We'll give the birds some time to move around a bit and give Mitzi something to sniff," I explained as I was spreading some chokecherry jelly on my fourth piece of toast. Dick's wife, Nancy, had sent a loaf of homemade bread along with us. It made great toast. I was thinking that this guy had all of the makings of an excellent hunting partner.

I had met Dick at a Wild Turkey Federation banquet some months earlier and learned that he was approaching retirement as personnel director of a large insurance company. We'd talked about fox hunting. Dick had been into that, some years back, and had been a hound owner. But then he got a bird dog. His daughter had brought Mitzi home one day, explaining that the poor thing needed a good home.

Since he found himself in the company of a two-year-old pointer of uncertain talent, Dick decided to try bird hunting with her. He dusted off his fox-hunting artillery, a 12 gauge Model 97 Winchester, and introduced Mitzi to pheasants on a game preserve.

"I don't think she'd ever been off a sidewalk before," he recalled, but Mitzi had enjoyed the hunt, and so had he. Before long, he had acquired armament more appropriate for the uplands, so both he and Mitzi were seasoned veterans of the pheasant fields before I met them.

Dick had confided that night that he really wanted to be a grouse and woodcock hunter. I said it was never too late to start, and agreed to show him where his dog might meet such birds. We had taken a trial run closer to home several days earlier and Mitzi had found and pointed a grouse. So now we were at a cabin I shared with some friends in northern Wisconsin, expectantly plotting against the "partridge," as ruffed grouse are known in those parts.

I was wondering where we should start. Some dim trails wind through those big woods. They lead to brush-bordered clearings where logging camps stood when the ridges echoed with thuds of axes and the crashing of giant pines. Left in the loggers' wake was a wasteland of huge stumps and tangled piles of slash. The land was reborn with a much different look. Large areas were soon dominated by aspens, pioneers in the natural succession of woodlands. Shrubs and briars also thrived on the sunlit forest floor.

Sparks struck by lightning or heedless men brought raging fires, fueled by the slash and fanned by gales of their own making. First here, then there, they blazed annually for decades. Each time, however, the woods rebounded with new vigor. The result was a tremendous boon for forest game, such as white-tailed deer and ruffed grouse. When I was a boy, the "cutover country" was a mecca for hunters from the cities. Many of them took trains to little whistle-stop stations, whence some local entrepreneur would carry them by wagon or sleigh to a shack in the woods. More often than not, they found shelter in the remains of abandoned logging camps.

Those buildings are mostly memories now. Even the big, fire-scorched stumps are moldering away. However, the legacy of the loggers endures in many ways. There are still trails and clearings, each with names still remembered by a few: The Christman Highway, Mattoon's Camp, The Horse Barns, The Crossroads. Every section of the north country has an unwritten roll of such places.

The woods have aged in other ways. Eventually, after fire control programs were implemented, they went mostly to maple, oak and ironwood. However, patches of briars and popples

Dick Matthisen and Mitzi relax and look over the results of a morning jaunt in the north woods.

persisted. Virtually unchanged were swamps verdant with cedar or dark with spruce. Balsam firs still bordered the trails in places. A few white pines and hemlocks remained too, standing as loners or in small groves.

In time, one learns where to look for grouse in such a forest. We might try hunting along the creeks, where we surely would flush some woodcock from the alders, and likely some grouse as well. However, we weren't apt to see much in the still-dense foliage.

"We'll try Mickey's Trail," I decided at last. The trail leads to a cabin well back in the woods. Relatively wide and sometimes mowed, it invites a four-hour jaunt, round trip, through ever-changing cover. I told Dick that it was a walk I had taken many times with Chips, my recently departed springer spaniel sidekick, and it had seldom disappointed us in our quest for grouse.

The sun was whisking the frost away as we left the Jeep and started up the trail. Mitzi had never seen such woods, but her experience on pheasants stood her in good stead because the first grouse we met acted like ringnecks. They ran far and flushed wild. Of fifteen flushes counted in four hours, only six birds were actually seen and shot at. However, Dick had pocketed three of those—and each of them over Mitzi's points!

The afternoon was even better. First, we stopped to visit Harry Croy. I wanted Dick to meet this old friend, who had bought 320 acres of woods of hardscrabble farmland purely for the purpose of creating grouse and woodcock habitat. Some important scientific studies have been made on what Harry named the Lake Shirley Wildlife Study Area, and I could listen to his views for hours. However, we left in time to ramble through some ideal cover in the Park Falls area. A two-hour stroll produced fourteen flushes. We got shots at five and bagged three, two of which had been taken over Mitzi's points. The other was a wild-flushing bird that I had managed to scratch down at long range. Mitzi fetched it from a thicket where no mere human would have ever found it.

No doubt about it. Both Dick and Mitzi became full-fledged grouse hunters that day about a decade ago. Dick was to learn, too late to avoid addiction, that grouse were not always so easily found and would seldom fall so readily to our guns. Hopelessly smitten, he now spends most of the season at his own northern Wisconsin hideaway, called "The Grouse House."

He spends the remainder of the year in search of the perfect grouse and woodcock gun, and has looked farther than anyone I know. Having already acquired a 24 gauge double, he has been heard wondering aloud where he might get a 32 gauge.

Other German shorthairs have succeeded Mitzi, now long departed. In fact, her successor, Kirby, is already in semi-retirement. His replacement is a bouncy babe named Calypso.

The seasons do fly by. However, the shorter the years become, the less waiting we must endure between opening days. No season now is complete without time spent at Dick's camp. The company's always good, and Nancy's homemade bread still makes great toast.

The Old Professor

You've heard it before; maybe even said it:

"Those hotshot clay bird shooters may be able to bust a hundred in a row, but that don't make 'em any good on live game."

Well now, there may be some cases where that's a fact. It's true that live birds present a gunner with a lot more problems and angles than will ever be encountered in skeet or trapshooting. True too, that in just a few years of soaring popularity, sporting clays has moved away from imitating real hunting situations. Today there is too much emphasis on special equipment and what I regard as stunt shooting. Nonetheless, it is all good practice, and if a good clay target shooter likes to hunt, it is usually bad news for gamebirds.

For evidence I would present Victor A. Reinders of Waukesha, Wisconsin, and his little black books. When I first met him some thirty years ago, Vic was already ranked among the greatest trapshooters of all time. A tall, lanky, bespectacled man with a ready smile, he then was a professor of chemistry at the University of Wisconsin in Milwaukee. He retired in 1972.

A complete list of Vic's achievements would require a separate chapter in this book, so suffice it to say that he has won several national titles, including the Clay Target Championship at the Grand American, and has been installed in the National Trapshooting Hall of Fame. He also was a member of the All-American trapshooting team for twenty-one years—eighteen of them in succession and four of them as captain—and was the first

Vic Reinders, trapshooter and grouse hunter, with his famous Model 31 Remington (Ned Vespa photo)

trapshooter ever to maintain an average of 98% or higher for 100,000 rounds. He then set another record by keeping it up for another 40,000.

But now meet Vic Reinders, grouse hunter and chronicler of facts. Since 1927, Vic has kept meticulous records of his gunning, whether shooting at clay or feathers, and they add up to some interesting reading. He has a detailed accounting of every shot he has fired in the sixty-eight ensuing years. They include some 981,000 rounds fired through a Remington Model 31 pumpgun that he bought second-hand in 1933. The total keeps changing because Vic is still shooting at age eighty-eight.

Vic's clay bird records have always been an open book, but it was with reluctance that he finally opened his hunting diaries to me.

"I'm afraid that people will look at the numbers and think I'm a game hog," he explained. However, when assured that they would be presented in the proper context, he began thumbing through the pages:

"Actually, I've shot more ducks than anything else," he began. Grouse are second, even though they are what I hunted the hardest for many years. So far, I've bagged 1,143 of them."

Not bad for a gunner who never saw a grouse until he was in his 20s and who did virtually all of that gunning during a 35-year period when he was commuting to the grouse woods each weekend from Milwaukee—a 400-mile round trip on average. Furthermore, he always skipped opening weekend because "there were too many leaves on the trees and too much traffic from the 'taxi' hunters."

Considering that he was hunting in lean years as well as good, in short seasons as well as long, and during some years with daily bag limits of three or four instead of the current five, his tally indicates that Vic can tell us some things about grouse hunting. And one of those things is that consistent success takes a lot of effort.

"Tommy and I have had a lot of grouse dinners, but we worked up quite an appetite getting them," he recalled. His wife Tommy was Vic's usual hunting partner, and a top trapshooting contender herself, until vision problems began to plague her several years ago. The couple never owned a dog, but sometimes hunted with friends who did.

"My records show that I averaged three miles of walking for every grouse I got over the years," Vic declared. He wasn't just guessing about that either. "I wore out a pedometer while hiking for grouse," he explained.

Hiking is hardly the word for it. I can tell you that Vic's favorite grouse hunting routes required mile after mile of bulldozing through alder tangles and romping through briar patches. I remember visiting with him and Tommy in their motel room after a hard day's hunt about thirty years ago. Both were busy with fabric cement, gluing more patches on their tattered canvas pants and coats.

"If you're working the right kind of cover, it's hard on clothes," Vic recalled. "In those days, I'd wear a pair of hunting pants right off to the boot tops in one season. I liked to stay down along the little creeks. That's the best bet for grouse. But I've found 'em just about every damn place you can think of, even cornfields. The one place you never have to look is in the big timber."

He recalled one day when he and Tommy bagged their limit of ten grouse with just fifteen shells.

"I think that's the best we did. I always figured a good average was three shells for one grouse, counting all shots on birds that took more than one shot to bring down," he said. "I never really went after woodcock; just took them incidental to grouse. They're harder to hit than pheasants, but fairly easy when they head straight up—if you wait until they level off. The ruffed grouse is a much tougher target, the hardest upland bird to hit consistently without a doubt," he declared.

Another thing that Vic is certain of is this: Gunning pressure has little to do with grouse populations—at least not in the big covers he always hunted. In 1964 he wrote an article titled "Partridge Aren't Shot Off!" for the Wisconsin Conservation Bulletin. Replete with statistical tables and graphs derived from years of entries in his little black books, the piece demonstrated that, if a hunter got away from the roads, flush rates of grouse did not decrease significantly as the season progressed.

His data indicated that the brush-busting hunter could expect to find virtually as many grouse at the end of a season as at the beginning. In contrast, he recorded abrupt declines in grouse seen on and near the roads during the first two weeks of the season.

"People who never get very far into the woods think the grouse are gone," he concluded. "The grouse population seems to be in no danger of overgunning through the agency of long open seasons."

Vic agreed, in a later interview, that intensive gunning pressure might depress grouse populations in farm woodlots and

Vic Reinders pages through one of his hunting journals.

other relatively accessible areas, but never, he emphasized, in the big woods of the north or the rugged hill and coulee country of Wisconsin's western counties.

Vic's views on guns and gunning are of interest too. Although he grew up on a farm near Mallard, Iowa, he was not allowed to carry a firearm until he was nearly sixteen. He says he had worn out two or three BB guns by then. (That could have been a good start. See the chapter on wingshooting.)

He was a high school senior before he got his first gun, a single shot .22 rifle, and upon graduation he got his first shotgun, a single shot .44 caliber smoothbore on the Stevens "Favorite" action.

"They only loaded shells with 5s and 8s," he remembers. "The Winchester shells held about a third of an ounce. Remington made a .44XL load that held a little more shot in a cardboard, bullet-shaped container that extended from the brass. I shot plenty of rabbits and pheasants with those."

A machinist friend later reamed the .44's chamber to accept 2-1/2-inch .410 shells. It was not until he had graduated from college and had a teaching job that Vic was able to replace it with something better. He paid $22.48 for a Western Field 12 gauge pumpgun with a 32-inch full-choke barrel. That was in 1930.

He had his introduction to trapshooting at the Milwaukee Gun Club in 1933 and broke 61 of 100. He decided that he liked the game, but not the gun. He bought his now legendary Remington for $50 that same year. A plain trap model with a 28-inch, full-choked barrel and ventilated rib, it would have cost $86 new.

He won his first state championship in 1938. Five years later, while training Air Force gunners in Texas, he won the state title there too. For years he also used the same gun for hunting, but during the 1940s he picked up another Model 31 just like the first (the serial numbers are only 124 apart). He also bought another barrel, skeet bored, and used that for most of his upland gunning thereafter. When primarily after ducks, he used the full choke barrel, but carried some "popcorn" loads for hikes through grouse coverts along the way.

He devised the loads himself, after finding more conventional spreader loads too complex and time-consuming to assemble. He used one of the old H-wads over the powder, then a 1/4-inch felt filler followed by an ounce of No. 7-1/2 shot and a half-inch layer of unpopped popcorn before crimping.

"Mixing the popcorn with the shot won't work. It has to be on top," he emphasized. I get a nice, even pattern—the same swath with the full choke barrel as I get with regular loads in the skeet barrel—and I've killed quite a few grouse with them. I always use 7-1/2s in my regular grouse loads too, either an ounce or 1-1/8 ounce."

Vic's attitude on guns is just as unpretentious. The last time I saw his old Remington, it was missing about four inches of its ventilated rib.

"It doesn't matter. I don't pay any attention to sights, and it doesn't show when I'm looking down the barrel anyway, " he said.

There also was a slight bulge in the barrel about two inches from the muzzle.

"I don't know when that happened. Somebody else called my attention to it several years ago. It doesn't seem to bother the patterns," he said with a shrug.

After spewing more than thirty tons of lead, the bore remains bright. Vic never runs a cleaning rod through it, "except to show somebody it doesn't need it," but he does recommend a bit more care for guns subject to the weather and wear and tear of hunting conditions.

Some other tips from a longtime teacher of gunners and student of grouse:

"I tell beginners to get one decent gun—a good 12 gauge pump—and learn how to shoot it. If you want to use it for more than one kind of hunting, just buy another barrel instead of another gun. I don't like changeable chokes.

"Instead of buying fancy guns, use the money for ammunition and practice. Almost any gun is better than the person shooting it. Spend some time shooting clay birds and you'll be a lot farther ahead as a wingshot," he concluded.

Take it from the old chemistry professor. That's a formula for success.

5

Thoughts on Dogs

The Dogless Hunter

Of all upland gamebirds, the ruffed grouse is probably the easiest to take without a dog.

Considering all that has been said and written about the challenges of grouse gunning, that may sound like a contradiction. Note, however, that I have not said that it is *easier* than with a dog, or that it is easy at all. I'm simply observing that an experienced hunter has a good chance of "walking up" a ruffed grouse. In fact, there are gunners with lots of grouse to their credit who'd *rather* hunt without a dog. If their experience has been limited to hunting with somebody's undisciplined, bumbling mutt, I don't blame them.

I've tried it both ways. It may sound dumb, but it usually takes me quite a while to get over the loss of a dog and start thinking seriously about committing to another. Also, there have been years when circumstances prevailed against me owning a dog. Sometimes then, I hunted with the dogs of companions, but often too, I hunted alone, relying wholly on my own senses to locate the birds. Such exercises are almost sure to make one a better grouse hunter.

To be consistently successful, the dogless hunter has to be a diligent student, learning everything possible about the grouse in the environs he hunts. He should know what they are likely to be eating, and when. He should understand where they are most apt to rest and roost. Equally important, he needs a sense of where they will want to fly when flushed. When you can put it all together, the triumph is sweet.

Now let's picture a brisk early autumn morning. Dew is glistening on the brown brackens as you start down an old tote road. Up ahead, there is a stretch where the sun is beginning to filter through shimmering aspen leaves, dappling the trail with dancing light. At that point, a dense cedar stand comes within fifty yards or so of the trail. You're quite sure that some grouse have roosted there, as they have often done before. You're confident too, that they have been moseying out to the trail during the past hour. Bright red wintergreen berries might invite a few pecks along the way, but the birds will want to breakfast on a fresh salad of clover and strawberry leaves while soaking up some early sun.

Walking stealthily through the dew-dampened woods, you stop often, looking and listening intently. You peer around a bend. Ah, is that a grouse sixty yards down the trail? What now? You want him to duck back into the undergrowth, so show yourself slowly. He doesn't move. Take a few steps forward. Still no movement. Are you sure that's a grouse? Just a few steps more. Ah, there he goes. He sneaked off the trail right near that broken popple. You move ahead now, unhurried. Near that popple, you stop again. Get ready.

Sometimes there's a rustling, sometimes even a few nervous "purts" as you wait, heart thumping. The chill morning air is suddenly much thinner, causing you to breath deeper, faster. Then there is that always surprising explosion of motion and emotion as a grouse rockets away. It veers toward the sanctuary in the cedars. Your shot is pure reflex. The bird plummets down. You mark the spot, but wait a few more heartbeats before going over to pick it up. You are still alert, expectant.

Another bird explodes from some hazelbrush bordering the trail, but it disappears in a blur of brown and yellow foliage as you turn and shoot. You listen hopefully for the soft thump that means dead grouse. There is none. Quickly reloading, you close the breech as still another grouse rises from that same hazel clump, not fifteen yards away. The bird actually flies into the clear and whirs right down the trail. Still you miss the first shot. The second? You're not sure. The grouse disappeared into the sun, which is now peeking above the trees. But listen. There is the sound of wings fluttering against the forest floor.

You'll do no more shooting now, until two downed grouse are recovered. The first takes some searching because you lost your mark when the others flushed. Your spent shells lie in the trail as a marker. You walk a line to the cedars, searching for signs. Not even a feather. You zig-zag slowly back and stand near the spent shells, trying to recreate the bird's flight in your mind. It all happened so fast. Maybe it was veering to the right faster than you thought. The second sweep is successful. The grouse is lying breast down, wings partly outstretched, hard to see. You pick it up reverently, smoothing its feathers, admiring the simple elegance of a mature gray cock grouse.

The second one is easy. Your ears had practically pinpointed its landing place, just inside the woods. A young hen. Doubtless there are more of her kin around, so you'll want to give this place another kick on the way back to the road. But first, you want to poke along a little alder-bordered creek over the next knoll, then amble down to those thornapples beyond. You can see already that this is going to be one of those days for the book.

The scene we've just played through your imagination was part of an actual hunt along a trail I've come to know well. I used it to illustrate some things:

Because I knew something about the cover, the terrain, and the grouse therein, I felt sure that at that time of day, the birds would be either on the trail or somewhere between it and the cedars. Even if I had not seen that first bird, I would have stopped for a while at several points along that same stretch. The young birds in the hazelbrush probably would have flushed at my approach, but, had he not been unnerved by my stopping, that old cock would have let me walk right by.

I stayed on the trail because it provided the best visibility and the quietest approach. Also, I could pretty much concentrate on looking to only one side. Odds were that any grouse flushed at that time were going to be to my right, between me and the cedars.

If someone had been with me, one of us would have stayed parallel to the trail while skirting the cedars. If hunting with a dog, I'd probably still have been walking the trail while keeping the dog quartering in the direction of the conifers. Later in the day I'd be in the brush with the dog, watching both ways.

If the day had dawned dark or drizzly, I would have set out somewhat later, and if it were raining hard, I'd have stayed in the cabin. In winter, I would have been looking in the hardwoods on the other side of those cedars. The grouse would likely be nipping catkins from the ironwoods then.

Similar scenarios can be drawn for all kinds and combinations of covers, be they alder runs or ridgetops. Each calls for different strategies, but all demand some intimate knowledge of the lifestyle of the resident grouse. Anyone can blunder into some grouse here and there when their numbers are up, but to find them consistently, through thick and thin, is a skill that does not come quickly or easily.

A dogless grouse hunter should figure on putting plenty of mileage on his boots. However, there's a lot more to hunting than the hiking. First, know what the birds are apt to be eating, and where that food can be found. Then remember that grouse gravitate to places where different kinds of cover converge. Corners. Pockets. Patches. Edges. Those are places where you should stop, look and listen.

Listening often pays off. I have been alerted to the presence of grouse by the sound of pattering feet on a still day, and have also often heard them fly into trees when taking alarm at my presence. That is a brief, fluttering sound—much different than either a panic flush or a hushed departure—and it tells you the approximate location of an alerted bird.

Drumming also announces the whereabouts of a grouse, of course, and it is not unusual to hear it on autumn days. Attempting to get a shot at that particular bird may prove to be a waste of time, but it doesn't hurt to try. At least you will be hunting to, and through, places where grouse hang out.

Teaming up with one or two partners who know what they're doing will improve the gunners' odds greatly, but grouse gunning without a dog is still a real challenge. I mentioned earlier that it had taught me some things. Especially, it has taught me even more appreciation of my dog!

One study at the Sandhill Wildlife Demonstration Area in central Wisconsin revealed that hunters using dogs bagged fourteen grouse per one hundred hours of effort, on average, compared to only six birds for a dogless hunter in the same period of time. Those with dogs were also shown to be more persistent, averaging four hours of effort per trip, compared to two hours for those without dogs.

That may have been because the dog owners were more dedicated hunters, but it also could be that flushing and bagging more grouse gave them added incentive to stay in the woods.

I suppose the day is not far off when one can buy a pocket-sized infrared heat sensor capable of locating something as small as a recently-expired timberdoodle. Then, since such a device could also locate live birds, why would anyone want to bother with a real dog?

Just ask the man who owns one.

Are Good Dogs Rare?

"Don always has good dogs," I overheard Jim say one morning at the Kernel Cafe. We were at the monthly breakfast meeting of a bunch of old-timers whimsically named "The Junior League," and, as usual, there were several conversations in progress at once. Bill Smeltzer was talking about the wild turkeys down his way, Norm Behrents was holding forth on fishing, Whitey Stewart was describing a fox hunt and Lloyd Swesey was expounding on bunny hunting with beagles.

Because I'd heard my dog's name mentioned, I was trying to tune in on what Jim Mense was saying. However, someone asked me a question right then, so I never heard the rest of the tale Jim was spinning. I started thinking about his comment later though. It was true, but surely not remarkable. Virtually all dogs are good dogs. You just have to determine what they're good at.

Don't think I'm being facetious. I'm just not "dog"matic about dogs. I'm well aware that what I say here will not jibe with most conventional advice and I am sorry if my views on the subject will give anyone the running fits. However, there are too many unhappy dogs and unhappy dog owners out there, all because of unrealistic expectations of canine perfection. The syndrome is most evident among grouse hunters, and particularly those who favor the pointing breeds. Each to his own tastes, I say. Just don't tell me that I'd be having a better time if my dog never pointed a rabbit and was invariably steady to wing and shot.

Mind you, I'm not saying that the experts are wrong. I count a number of well-known dog trainers, dog writers, and field trial folks among my friends and have no arguments with whatever gets them the results they want. However, I'm here to tell you what has worked just fine for me, with dogs of varied and sometimes obscure ancestry.

Gun at ready, Don Johnson advances through dense September cover as Chips quarters ahead in quest of grouse. (Sherman Gessert photo)

Most authorities advise us to get rid of a dog that doesn't meet our high expectations. Their reasoning is sound. Why spend ten years of your life afield with a failure? But what are you supposed to do when the pup has already become a member of the family? I think that most hunters are like me. You get a pup and you're stuck with it until death do you part. And, since most hunters own no more than one dog at a time, you have two choices: go afield with something less than a canine paragon, or leave your dog at home.

You also may have heard or read that good grouse dogs are the rarest of finds. I'm reminded of the old canard about a man being entitled to only one good woman and one good dog in a lifetime. Having been married to the same good woman for forty-five years, I can't speak with any authority on their general availability. However, I *can* assure you that most dogs have the makings of good hunters, if not great ones. And that goes for grouse dogs too.

It certainly does help to get a dog from proven lineage and of a breed well-suited to the kind of hunting you plan to do. Most dogs are pretty versatile, but you wouldn't pick an English setter if you spend most of your time in a duck blind or a Chesapeake retriever if woodcock are your favorite quarry. Your best bet is to get a dog whose parents are proven in the line of work you have in mind for it.

Irrespective of breeding, there is one thing that I regard as absolutely essential if you are to train your own dog. It must be completely devoted to you. It is not really necessary to buy the dog as a pup to get that kind of connection. Even a mature dog will bond to a new owner. It is vital, however, that it has been socialized at an early age and has a happy, outgoing attitude around humans. Training a dog that acts fearful or ill-at-ease is a tough task for a professional, to say nothing of the average owner.

But let's pause right here to get a couple of things straight: Although I like to hunt with dogs and enjoy their company, I don't think that everyone must or should have one. Nor do I think that everyone should try to be a dog trainer. Owning dogs entails a considerable commitment. It is costly and time-consuming. They need care, affection, and exercise. Training them right takes a prodigious amount of time and patience. Shortcuts can backfire badly and are best left to the pros. There are some excellent books available on dog training and I recommend them to anyone who wants detailed advice on the subject. All I want to impart here is a philosophy.

A dog that loves you will want to please you, but it first must know just what it is that you want it to do. That takes more than

The author's 12 gauge Ithaca SKB and his old springer spaniel, Chips—the combination that has accounted for more grouse than any other in Johnson's long hunting career. (George R. Cassidy photo)

demonstration and encouragement. It takes patience. You have to wait until the dog does something right, then lavish it with praise and perhaps a treat. Don't wait until the performance is perfect. Praise the pup when it sniffs a grouse wing, when it picks it up, when it carries it toward you. Celebrate when it finally delivers anything at all to hand on the command "fetch." Let the dog know that it has done something truly great.

On the other hand, if the dog is disappointing you, let him know it. You don't have to shout or speak angrily. Use a disapproving tone. Walk away. He'll get the message, and the next time he may try to do better. Once you are sure that the dog knows what you want it to do, it's all right to get a little more stern when it goofs. However, continue to accent the positive. Keep praising the right moves and try to keep it fun. It's called positive reinforcement, and it works.

A dog is genetically programmed to do some of the things you want. A tiny pointer pup may lock up at the sight of a butterfly and a little Labrador retriever may fetch a glove almost as soon as it can waddle. Encourage, but don't push, a precocious pup.

To some extent, you can select the traits you want by careful choice of the parentage. However, pedigrees aren't performance contracts. Every dog is different; some are smarter than others, some have better noses. Some have an inborn desire to run, others like to putter. When you acquire a pup, you really don't know which way it will go, and long before you have a clue as to its capabilities, your kids have named it and your wife is knitting it a sweater. What to do? You can play the hand you've been dealt for all it is worth. You adapt.

When you think about it, that's no more than fair. Each of us is different too. Just as our dogs must adapt to our idiosyncrasies, we should adjust to theirs. Every dog has its strong points. Identify them and go with them. I have had pointing dogs and flushing dogs, purebred and mongrel. With each of them, I found myself altering my hunting style to better fit that dog's talents. In time, we became a real team and I had another "good dog."

The same approach holds when you get an adult dog. It may have been trained in just the manner you want, but there still is a period of mutual adjustment before you are communicating completely. It is important to learn how to "read" the dog, picking up on the meanings of its every action and gesture. No two act exactly the same. At the same time, our dogs are also "reading" us. When you can communicate on that wavelength, it isn't necessary to be constantly "hacking" a dog with voice and whistle.

Brighton, the author's shorthair, points to a tangle of brush, vines and windfalls where a grouse is hiding. Grouse-wise dogs learn that such spots are always worth investigating.

Even if your dog has been professionally trained, it is important for you to remind it periodically of what it is supposed to do, and how. Combine a walk with a brief refresher course on the basics, which are, "Whoa," "Sit," "Stay," "Come," "Fetch" and "Heel." Remember to praise a good performance too. The most frequent complaint I hear from professional trainers is that their clients allow their dogs to lapse into bad habits, thereby undoing what was accomplished at the kennel.

It has often been said that an exceptional grouse dog isn't so hot on woodcock, and that pheasants will ruin a dog for either. I don't believe that. It probably had more validity back in the old days, when neither woodcock nor grouse were so apt to run and flush wild as they are today.

My present partner, Brighton, is as good a grouse and woodcock dog as I could ever want. When she has a bird nailed, she is a statue. Nothing will budge her. If the bird is moving off slowly, she waits for my approach, then proceeds cautiously, relocating again and again until the quarry is either pinned down or (unavoidable at times) flushed wild. However, if she perceives that the bird is running, my dog will often break point and make a wide half-circle, running pell-mell until well ahead of the runner. Then she loops back to "cut it off at the pass." Often the tactic works and the befuddled bird is pinned at last. Pheasants taught Brighton that move.

I am well aware that what I have just described is not exactly classic behavior. However, I tend to be pragmatic about things that accomplish the desired ends. On the other hand, I wouldn't mind at all if Brighton were steady to wing and shot in the coverts. It's a nice touch, and it has some practical value as well. Every season I pass up a number of grouse shots (and even a few at woodcock) because the bird has gone out low and my dog (or someone else's) is bolting after it. I refrain from shooting at low birds. Even if the dog isn't in the line of fire, there's a possibility of it being peppered by shot glancing from a branch. I've only seen that once and no lasting harm was done, but I don't care to see it again.

I have not troubled to train Brighton further because (1) teaching steadiness to wing and shot is neither easy nor much fun for either trainer or trainee, and (2) when hunting pheasants, I want her to get out there fast, like an infielder calling for a pop fly ball. If a ringneck hits the ground with its legs still locomoting, a dog needs all the edge it can get.

I do like a dog that hunts close, be it a pointer or a flusher. However, those who prefer a fast, wide-ranging pointing dog will get no argument from me—so long as that dog is biddable and hunts always with and for its owner, instead of for itself.

A dog ought to adjust its range to the cover, keeping in frequent visual or audio contact with its owner or handler. Unless making game or on point, Brighton checks on my whereabouts frequently. In dense, early-season covers she rarely ranges farther than my aging ears can hear the tinkle of her bell. On the western prairies she'll make much wider sweeps, so long as she can turn and see me now and then. That is my ideal. You are welcome to have another.

Although I have talked mainly about pointing dogs, I think that the average grouse hunter might be best served by a flushing dog these days. Brighton's predecessor was a sturdy springer spaniel. My constant companion for more than a decade, he became a legend in his own time. I still am meeting people in my travels who have recollections of Chips doing this or Chips doing that. Nobody who ever saw him hunt will forget him, for he did his work well indeed. He hunted reasonably close, had a choke-bored nose, and hit the toughest cover with absolute abandon. He had boundless enthusiasm for everything we did and would retrieve anything from anywhere. A dog like that can make its owner look pretty good.

Brighton pointing a grouse which is just about to flush a few feet from her nose.

Brighton returns happily with the first grouse of a new season.

Take Your Pick

I think that good grouse dogs are found among many breeds. Because versatility is a virtue for those of us who hunt other species, many of my friends own springers. Others, who also do more duck hunting, use Labrador retrievers in the uplands. I don't hold with the idea that a retriever is useful only to fetch birds after a pointer has made the finds. A close-quartering Lab is a good grouse-getter. And what's more, I think that pointing dogs should fetch their own birds.

In areas I frequent, the Brittany spaniel and German shorthair have been gaining in popularity, reflecting an increasing preference for closer-working dogs. With some exceptions, the traditional setters tend to range widely. There is nothing prettier than a fine setter though, in motion or on point, and I expect that they're going to be around as long as there are grouse to hunt and people to hunt them. Whatever your preference, pick a dog from solid grouse-hunting stock. Then say a prayer. There are bird dogs and bird brains in every breed.

Long hair or short? Nobody has yet bred a dog with the perfect covering for working the coverts, so you make your choice. Brighton's coat is as sleek as a seal's, sparing me from many hours of removing burrs each season, but she also is subject to more cuts and scratches than a longer-haired breed would suffer. Spaniels and setters can run through thorn and briar and emerge virtually unscathed, but their coats are veritable magnets to any sticktights they touch.

If you own a spaniel, its a good idea to have its coat clipped before the hunt begins. The fur and feathering will grow back in plenty of time to provide winter warmth, and by that time, stickers are less of a problem. Setters just don't look right without their plumed tails and feathered legs though, so they seldom are treated to September trims. Their beauty also causes them another problem. That lovely, undocked tail takes a terrible beating in rough cover, and, once it has become raw and bloody it is a hard thing to cope with. There is no harder thing to keep bandaged than the tip of a busy setter's tail.

If you hunt during the snowy times, foot problems are another thing to think about. Long-haired dogs are more apt to be troubled with ice balls building up between their toes. It usually happens when the snow is a little tacky, and it can be a real problem. The dog may stop hunting frequently to chew at the ice, and may

A Labrador retriever poses proudly with a South Dakota sharptail. Flushing dogs that work within gun range are good choices for gunning on the prairies, and their retrieving skills are welcome there too.

Ned Vespa pauses to praise his young setter, Gracie, after a successful morning hunt in Wisconsin's north woods.

ultimately become too footsore to continue. I have tried trimming the hair between the toes, then applying various kinds of lubricant, such as petroleum jelly, to keep the ice from adhering. (You have to take care with what you use, because the dog will lick it off, sooner or later.) Nothing seemed to help much. I also have tried boots of rubber and buckskin with poor results on snow, although the rubber boots have served well enough for hunts on prickly prairies.

A long-haired dog, or any with a heavy undercoat, certainly is better adapted to cold than are the pointers. However, shorthairs keep warm enough when actually hunting, even if the windchill is hovering around 0°F. They do, of course, need more protection from the cold when they are inactive.

You should make a list not only of what you expect, but what you would not accept in a canine companion. Not only will that help you choose a dog, but it will help you decide when one is just not worth keeping. There are two things I will not abide, but fortunately, I have never had to give up on a dog because of either of them. One is a dog that runs wild, hunting for its own pleasure, and chasing up birds forty acres away. The other is a dog that will not fetch from water. Even grouse and woodcock are dropped into ponds or streams sometimes, and I'll be switched if I'm going to swim out for them while the dog watches from shore.

I think that shock collars are too often used as a quick-fix, and I have never used one. However, I would have welcomed such help in instructing a long-ago Brittany, had such gadgets been invented then. At the time, I knew little about dog training, and virtually nothing about pointing dogs. Specks eventually did come around to my way of thinking and he found his niche as a flushing dog and a duck retriever. A darned good one too. I can imagine the shudders and snickers that admission has evoked, but hey, we got a lot of birds. I guess my motto is, "Whatever works."

At least I am not alone in that way of thinking. Some years ago I was judging flushing dogs at a hunting dog trial on a large game preserve. There was a big turnout, and everybody was having a fine time. The course ran through a complex of excellent cover, and several quail and pheasants were being planted before each brace was run. Each entrant was allowed to work his dog until he was satisfied that his dog had hunted it thoroughly, and each could keep as many birds as he could bag. Since none of the early participants collected all of their birds, there was quite an accumulation of quail and pheasants out there waiting for a good shot with a good dog.

About midmorning a man showed up with an Irish setter that he insisted upon entering as a flushing dog. There was no rule against that, but since we didn't want the setter running with a spaniel or a retriever, we put him off until we took our lunch break. In the meantime, another Irish setter, maybe ten months old, was also entered as a flusher. I hid my amusement. I didn't have a high regard for the breed because, for too long, it had been bred for beauty instead of brains. (In recent years there has been a comeback of hunting stock and some good red setters are being seen.)

"Well," I told the other judge, "we've got two of 'em now, so I guess it's off to the races."

As soon as we took to the field, it was apparent that the young dog knew nothing, and its owner even less, about what it was supposed to be doing. Ah, but the man with the older dog! They were a sight to watch. They worked the cover to perfection, the dog quartering within gun range and always signaling when a flush was imminent. The guy could shoot too. His coat was bulging with more than a dozen birds when he called it quits. In competition with some fine flushing dogs, that setter took the second place trophy. You just never know. They're even breeding pointing Labrador retrievers these days.

Canine Compatibility

The compatibility of canines is a problem with hunting dogs that I have seldom seen addressed. Two hunters may be the best of buddies, but if their dogs don't get along—or even if they just don't hunt well together—there is trouble. Friendships can be severely strained.

Fights are the most serious problem. My springer, Chips, had only a couple of real brawls in his life. He was a big dog, strong and self-assured, and he ignored most challenges. One time, however, he and Bill Stokes's springer, Doc, got into one of those frays where all you can see is a whirlwind of flying fur, gnashing teeth and flashing eyeballs. It caught us by surprise. We had just emerged from the woods after a couple of hours of grouse hunting, during which both dogs had hunted well and without any apparent animosity. Poor Doc was considerably the worse for wear by the time we managed to pull them apart. Bill, understandably

Jessie and Brighton team up to pin down a woodcock in a thicket. Teamwork like this is a joy to watch, but competitiveness between dogs can be a problem.

perturbed, thereupon declared that he preferred not to hunt with anyone who used a rhinoceros instead of a dog. Our friendship survived, but those two dogs never hunted together again.

Other kinds of conflicts can be more subtle. Some dogs work well together; others compete. Yours might regularly honor the points of one dog, yet try to steal points from another. Hunters really attuned to their dogs should soon see what's going on and take appropriate action. That may mean hunting separately, or, if continuing to hunt together, using only one of those dogs at a time. There is no point in making accusations or excuses on either side. Interrelationships between dogs are often beyond our ken. A dog has a reason for everything that it does, but the reason is frequently a mystery to us.

It is generally thought that conflicts are certain if pointing dogs and flushing dogs are hunted together, but, as I've already related, that is not always the case. I learned that years ago, after Ed Scherer showed up with an eighteen-month-old English setter named Joe. Ed brought him back from a quail hunt in East Texas, doubtless leaving a rancher chuckling about the deal. Virtually every ranch in Texas quail country has a few setters around. They rarely have papers. Their performance is their pedigree. Joe had been exposed to a lot of quail, but he didn't range as far or run as hard as those Texans expected him to. I suppose some would have called him a plodder.

Ed knew what he was doing, however. One of Joe's predecessors was another Texas-born setter named King, who did himself proud in Wisconsin coverts. Ed just brought that close-working setter home, set him down in proper cover, and had an instant grouse and woodcock dog.

Joe was slow for a setter, but the birdiest dog you'd ever want to see. And steady. His contemporary in my kennel was Chips. Since Ed and I often hunted together, the setter and the springer became well-acquainted, and even partners on running birds. It worked like this:

While working the same covert, Ed and I hunted separately, but within shouting distance. Occasionally then, I'd hear Ed shout, "Bring Chips over here! We've got another runner!"

There would be Joe, in ultra-cautious pursuit of a perambulating partridge. Point and creep. Point and creep. He always seemed to breathe a sigh of relief when Chips showed up. Then, as Ed and I moved into position, Chips would take the track, flush the bird, and make the retrieve if necessary. Good old Joe didn't mind a bit. He was off looking for another grouse.

Beepers and Bells

The first time I ever hunted behind a dog with a beeper collar was in 1971 when Nick Sisley came out from Pennsylvania with his fine little pointer, Grouse Magic. We had a good hunt, and Magic lived up to her name, but I have to admit that the beeper bothered me. Those early models offered no options. They beeped all the time with the interval between beeps changing when the dog stopped. It seemed too high-tech to me—too much like signals from a circling satellite—but the idea certainly had possibilities.

I wrote the maker of that beeper, suggesting that he make his creation sound like a bell. I didn't know anything about electronics, but I figured if an electric chord organ could be made to sound like a mandolin, he could sure convert a beep into a bell. The letter I got back told me, quite succinctly, to mind my own business. I haven't offered my services to a beeper-maker since, and I guess that's why they still haven't gotten them right.

I've tried several kinds of beepers and I use one regularly until the foliage is down. It saves me a lot of time otherwise wasted looking for my dog on point. I like to go grouse hunting, not dog hunting. I use them strictly in the point-only mode, and still rely on a bell to keep track of the dog's whereabouts. I'd just much rather listen to a bell.

The beeper I use the most can be set to sound like a hawk cry. That's supposed to freeze a bird in its tracks. I have observed no such effect, but I use the hawk cry anyway. It sounds better than a beep.

I am going to tell you what to look for in a beeper, and why, but I can't tell you where to find it. Nobody yet makes one with all of the features I'll mention:

•It ought to sound like a bell. If they can make a chord organ...(Oh, I guess I said that already.)

•It should direct the sound away from the dog's ears. (No explanation needed.)

•Options should include settings for "point only," and the interval between when the dog stops and the signal starts should be adjustable. (Because that's the way they ought to be.)

Brighton, wearing a beeper, poses after a morning's work. The gun us an AYA 20.

•It should be adjustable both for tone and volume. (Not all of us can hear as well, or as wide a range of frequencies, as we once could.)

•It should be powered by readily-available and easily-replaceable batteries and should have a low-battery indicator. (Some of us are still hunting out of camps that don't have electrical outlets for recharging beepers.)

•It should *not* have a magnetic on-off switch. (A magnet is just one more thing you can forget or lose, and if you hang it on your whistle lanyard or keychain, sooner or later, it'll make your compass go bonkers.)

•It should be light and compact. (A hunting dog shouldn't have to look like a St. Bernard carrying a keg of brandy.)

•It should be watertight. (Even an upland dog is going to encounter creeks, ponds and puddles. I've had a beeper fizzle due to nothing more than a light rain or heavy dew.)

•It should sell for no more than _____ . (You fill in the blank. What would such a beeper be worth to you? Let your favorite beeper-maker know and maybe we'll get one like I've described, by and by.)

So much for beepers. I prefer a bell, and, as mentioned earlier, I still rely on one to follow my dog's movements. Out on the prairies where I can see my dog far off, or in winter, when visibility is much improved, I dispense with the beeper altogether and count on a blaze-orange reflective collar to help me locate my dog on point.

Sometimes, when the birds are especially spooky, I remove the bell too. I didn't used to think that a bell had much, if any, effect on the birds' behavior, but I've changed my mind. While hunting alone in central Wisconsin a few seasons ago, I had a day and a half when it seemed almost impossible to get within shooting range of a grouse. I could see that Brighton was doing her best, and was getting as frustrated as I was. She was not bumping birds. They simply were running and flying well ahead of us. I glimpsed a few, but most of them were only heard as they took off.

Then there was an added aggravation. Brighton lost her bell. Actually, the bell was still on her collar, but the clapper had dropped off, the hinge worn through by countless oscillations over the years. The cover was still heavy and it was hard to stay keyed on the dog without that bell, so we circled back towards the truck, where I had a spare.

Before I had gone one hundred yards, I heard Brighton's beeper beckoning. Another just-departed bird and another unproductive point, no doubt, but it had to be checked out. I was a little careless

Nick Sisley and Magic on a winter visit to the author's old Ace-In-The-Hole covert in northern Wisconsin

in my approach and was taken aback when a grouse whirred from the ground not fifteen feet from Brighton's nose. I missed with both barrels.

Inured to such disappointments, my dog romped out of sight and soon was pointing again, possibly at the same bird. Again the flush was just in front of the dog and that time I was prepared for it. I pocketed that grouse and another before reaching the road. A light was dawning. Why were the birds suddenly holding? Could it be the bell? I experimented the rest of the day, bell here, no bell there, and bagged one more bird in the process. While wearing the bell, Brighton was able to nail down just one bird in five attempts. Without the bell, she pegged two more and had just one wild flush. That convinced me that the bell made a difference, at least at that time and place.

It is probable that those birds had been hunted enough to associate the bell with approaching trouble. It is probable too that grouse elsewhere have made the same connection. These days I often carry the bell in a pocket, slipping it on Brighton's collar only when I really feel it is needed. I may miss its merry tinkle, but I'm loathe to give the grouse any more advantage than they already have.

Canine Care

Dogs should have routine medical checkups at least annually, and should be taken to a veterinarian promptly if you detect that something is seriously or mysteriously amiss. Most dogs are amazingly healthy and durable, but it sometimes seems that canines are subject to most of the maladies that plague humans, plus a whole litany of their own.

I once nearly lost a dog due to tetanus. I wasn't even aware that dogs could get it. I wanted to know why they aren't inoculated against it like we are. The vet said that it is very rare. Not a very good answer, I thought, when your dog is at risk of getting something that another shot could prevent.

Immunizations against Lyme disease are a must almost anywhere we take our dogs these days. I also spray the dog with a proven tick repellent when hunting in badly infested areas. I've tried various tick collars and don't trust them after finding live ticks dug in under them. Lyme disease helped shorten the life of my old springer, Chips. We didn't know what was ailing him. That was

Ed Erickson and his setter, Perp, take time out after a tough trek through dense early-season cover in Michigan's Upper Peninsula. Note that Perp is wearing a good-sized bell to help Ed keep tabs of her whereabouts.

before we knew much about the disease and we didn't realize dogs could get it.

Heartworm prevention is vital. Two or three decades ago we never worried about it in our northern latitudes, but it is an ever-present threat today unless a dog is protected. That is a lot easier than it used to be, because one dosage per month will do the trick instead of a pill each day. The dog has to have a blood test before starting the medication each spring, and that's a good time for a general checkup. The monthly medication must be maintained throughout the mosquito season.

Shots for prevention of rabies, canine parvo-virus and leptospirosis are among other things your dog requires on a regular schedule. I find it best to have a veterinary clinic keep track of such things and notify me of when they're due.

Using plain common sense will avoid some serious troubles in the field. One big mistake is to feed a dog heavily before hunting. The consequences can be severe. Instead, offer just a small portion of the dog's regular ration before hunting and save the remainder for later, after the dog has had a chance to settle down at the end of the hunt. It's fine to offer a hard-working dog a snack of something sweet during the hunt. No chocolate though.

It is important that the dog has ample water. Carry some with you when hunting in dry country. Thirsty dogs can quickly learn how to drink from those plastic bottles that runners and bikers use.

Especially watch for signs of heat stress. It is easy for dogs to overdo it in warm weather. They don't know when to quit. If you must hunt when it's hot, stop often for a rest, preferably in some shade. If the dog is salivating a lot and panting very heavily, check its gums. If they are dark red, you're already in trouble. Get the dog's body temperature down as soon as possible. If you can immerse it in water, do so. If there is no quick response, get to a vet. Heat stress can be deadly.

One of the things on my checklist for a hunting trip is "dog box." That does not refer to a box for my dog to sleep in, but one that contains a collection of pharmaceuticals and paraphernalia that could come in handy should my dog become sick or hurt. I am not going to give a complete list here because there are better sources. Ask your veterinarian what he or she recommends for a real canine first-aid kit. Mine includes the usual antiseptics, salves, tapes and bandages, peroxide to induce vomiting (if the dog is poisoned), and some basic tools like forceps, scissors, pliers, and nail clippers. There also are boots, extra collar, spare beeper, bells and such.

It's important that hunting dogs have frequent chances to drink, especially in warm weather. George Cassidy gives Jessie a refreshing swig of water after working a covert in early October.

Of course, the best thing to do when a dog is ill or injured is to get it to a veterinarian pronto, but that is not always possible. You should be prepared to handle emergencies yourself. Considering the hazards they are exposed to in their work, it's a wonder that dogs aren't hurt more often than they are. It's a rare year though, that I don't see a few more stitches being taken in Brighton's hide.

You have to pay attention. Hunting dogs tend to be stoics. Even seemingly pampered pets will often suffer painful injuries without complaint when their hunting blood is up. I once saw a little cocker spaniel trying to catch a muskrat that had been rambling overland between a couple of flowages. A muskrat is incredibly quick and its teeth are like scissors. The little cocker's face and ears were literally shredded before her owner came to the rescue, but she never whimpered. She just wanted to go back and try again.

Last year, Dick Matthisen noticed that his young shorthair, Calypso, was licking a paw after a day's hunt. He investigated and saw that something was embedded too deeply to be extracted without a vet's help. The pad yielded a 7/8-inch-long thorn, but it had not stopped the dog. It hadn't even slowed her down.

Just one more example: Early in the hunt three years ago, Brighton bounded down a hillside to fetch a woodcock Dick had dropped near a beaver pond. I thought I saw a red smear on her belly as she bounded away after delivering the bird. However, she was making game, so I let her go. She led me to a grouse. After she'd fetched it, I examined her injury. Not much blood was flowing, but there was a nasty-looking cut, with a flap of dangling skin. The hunt was over. I kept her at heel during the long hike to the road, although she wanted to hunt every foot of the way.

It took an hour to drive to the nearest veterinary clinic, where I learned that the injury was worse than the simple cut or tear I had thought. The vet's probe revealed a four-inch puncture angling obliquely into the rib cage. Had the angle been more direct, it could have been fatal.

A week later the drain tubes came out, and in a few days more, the stitches. Then we took off for North Dakota, where the sharptails were waiting. Brighton hit the prairie on the run. My wife sometimes thinks that we grouse hunters are nuts. But then, so are our dogs.

Wearing boots to protect her raw paws, Brighton pauses to rest on a hay bale during a week of hard hunting across a rough and prickly prairie.

Skunks and Porkies

Skunks and porcupines are characters that a hunter would just as soon ignore, but they have ways of attracting attention. Either of them may seem irresistible to a dog—at least once. Some dogs, after their first close encounter, will be cautious about approaching such unpleasantness again. Others will bear a grudge and attempt to even the score every time a skunk or porcupine is met. There is, of course, no way the dog can win. Even in death, the vanquished is victorious.

Diligent training can dissuade most dogs from such pursuits, just as they can be discouraged from showing too much interest in snakes, deer and other troublesome critters. However, this is about what to do when the worst occurs and you suddenly have a dog that looks like a pin cushion or is surrounded by a reeking cloud of skunk cologne.

Skunks first: Everybody knows what a skunk smells like and just about everybody knows about some surefire way to get rid of the stink. The trouble is, most of them don't work very well. Tomato juice? Charred cornmeal? Deodorant soap? No such exorcisms are very effective when a dog has really been doused.

A curious thing about dogs is that although their noses are far keener than ours, they seem to be only briefly troubled by their own reeking odor after being sprayed. The dog will usually rub its eyes (skunk spray smarts) and roll around in the grass a bit. Then it will go merrily on its way, looking puzzled and hurt if its owner acts aloof.

Vinegar or a weak solution of household chlorine bleach will be of some help in removing odors from pets or clothing, but what is needed is some magic potion that will kill the odor right away, before you must put a skunked dog in your vehicle and drive home with all windows open and your head hanging outside.

Since I discovered it in 1979, I have always had a bottle of "Skunk-Off" in my dog kit. It is not widely available, but your local veterinarian can probably tell you where to get it, or something like it. The de-skunker I use comes in a pocket-sized plastic bottle from which you can squeeze either a stream or a spray. The recommended procedure is to use the mist until you can move in closer. Then, if the skunk's shot was from short range, you can squirt the spot where the scent is most intense. That's all there is to it. The stuff is not odorless. It smells like cheap perfume, but it does tame the stench.

Now porcupines: You are apt to meet them almost anywhere—deep in the north woods, high in the mountains, even out on the prairies where there are few trees. If you spot one rustling along the ground before your dog does, you might want to snap on the leash, take the pup over there and tell it, in no uncertain terms, that porkies are not to be toyed with. If the dog makes the discovery first (the more usual scenario) the porcupine will make the same point, in spades.

It's somewhat scary to see your dog bristling with quills. Usually they are concentrated around the dog's head—in the lips and nose, inside the mouth and in the tongue. The dog is very unhappy. Its harpooned flesh is quivering with pain. What to do? Just pull 'em out, and the sooner the better!

You may have heard about ways to make that unpleasant task easier. The ones I've tried were a waste of time. In my experience, snipping the quills "to let them collapse" or twisting them to "screw them out" makes the job harder, if anything. However, if the very idea of causing such pain makes you wince, and if you're not far from home, here's a recipe I got long ago from an old-time woodsman who had lots of experience with hounds and porcupines:

"Make a solution of one cup vinegar and two teaspoons baking soda and stir well," Mike Plaza told me. "Then pat it on all exposed parts of the quills and wait ten minutes. Apply again and wait ten minutes more. The soda and vinegar solution softens the lime and calcium in the quills, causing them to shrink. Then you can pull them out with your fingers without hurting the dog."

I've never tried Mike's formula because I've never had the ingredients at hand when I needed them. The quills are not usually imbedded very deeply at first, but they have a nasty way of working in farther with every minute of delay. I therefore prefer to get right to work. Steady the dog as much as possible and begin pulling quills, one by one. If you are in porcupine country, you really ought to carry a pliers on your belt, but lacking that, you can do a pretty good job with your fingers. Pinch the quill as close to the dog as possible and yank it straight out. It is barbed and won't want to let go, so you can't be gentle, but be as careful as you can. Leaving a broken tip in the dog is unavoidable sometimes, but it can cause big trouble later.

There may be quite a bit of bleeding, especially when quills are being extracted from the tongue. Don't worry about that. It won't last long. The amazing thing is that a dog will forget the trauma in no time. Only minutes after having dozens of quills removed from tender parts of their anatomy, I have seen dogs hunting again as if nothing had happened.

Usually, a dog's first encounter with a quill pig is the worst, but some never seem to learn. I especially remember helping extract hundreds of quills from one Irish setter in two days' time. It was early spring, and Bob Dreis and I had planned a backpacking along the Ice Age Trail, which wends through northern Wisconsin. Bob is an old wilderness buddy, a retired state wildlife manager and former regional representative of the Ruffed Grouse Society.

An eager young photographer was assigned to accompany us for part of the trek, and when he learned that my springer sidekick was going along, he asked if his dog could go too. I explained that Chips carried his own supplies in a rig he wore like saddlebags, but if the photographer wanted to carry the extra grub, his dog was welcome.

The lad showed up heavily laden with cameras and lenses, accompanied by a happy-go-lucky setter. We got off to a good start. Chips was finding lots of grouse, buoying our expectations for the next autumn. The first spring flowers were appearing and the mosquitoes had not yet arrived. It looked like it would be a fun trip.

Not more than two miles into the hike, however, trouble reared its prickly tail. The setter met a porcupine and attacked it with zeal. When we arrived at the scene of the din, the porky was trying to shuffle away. However, the dog kept lunging at it, each time getting another whack of the porky's tail. Its tail was beginning to look like a 'possum's. The dog had most of its quills.

We took turns holding the struggling setter and pulling quills. It took a long time, but we did a pretty good job of it and set off again, confident that the dog had learned a lesson. Alas, he had not. I have never seen porcupines as numerous as they were that spring, and I lost count of that dog's encounters with them. After a couple of days we called a halt. The setter had to see a veterinarian. There were broken stubs of quills in its throat, and even its eye sockets.

Even a small part of a quill can work deep in time. There are stories of quills ultimately reaching vital organs and causing death. I know of one that crept around in a dog's head for four months before it made its presence known. Another dog might have complained sooner, but not Duke.

Duke is a powerfully-built shorthair who lives with Ned Vespa. He was a real junkyard dog when Ned got him, free of charge. George Cassidy brought him to Ned's place and assured him that Duke would be a hunting dog. "Never mind that crazy look he sometimes has in his eyes," George said.

Indomitable Duke's escapades have since become legend in our circle, but he did prove to be a hunter. In fact, he was working well on woodcock on the day he tried to eat the porcupine. Discouraged from that endeavor, he waited impatiently for a fistful of quills to be plucked from his face. Then he resumed hunting as if nothing had happened. That was in early October.

In February, Duke's head suddenly ballooned. Ned hauled him off to a veterinary clinic where it was discovered that a piece of porcupine quill was triggering a massive infection. It had been inching around in the dog's head all that while, looking for the best spot to wreak the porky's revenge.

I went along with Ned to pick Duke up after his surgery. It was a pitiful sight. Duke was all stitched and bandaged and there were drain tubes jutting from his skull, but he seemed as buoyant as ever. Ned didn't look nearly as happy when he looked at the bill. He stared at it for a while, blinking and swallowing, and finally said:

"This is a hell of a lot of money to spend on a free dog."

I'll never forget that vet's answer. It is one of the great truisms of life.

"There *are* no free dogs," he declared.

Traveling with Dogs

For years I spent much of my time on the road, and I still do a fair amount of traveling, usually with a dog. My dogs have stayed in countless motels, and even some classy hotels, where dogs were allowed on the elevators but not in the swimming pools.

I could count on my fingers the times I have been turned away because of my dog.

Innkeepers have told me that they have a lot less trouble with travelers' dogs than they do with tipsy guests and rowdy children. However, those who do have "No Pets" rules usually have good reasons. Here are some ways to avoid being one of those reasons.

Never sneak a dog into your room. I always mention the dog when calling ahead for a reservation, and I'm up-front about it when I pull into a place without advance notice. If the proprietor or desk clerk is skeptical, I say something like, "Would you like to see my dog? He (or she) is my regular traveling companion and we have never had a complaint." A tail-wagging introduction clinches it. Ask too, where the dog can be walked before bedtime, and before hitting the road the next day. Usually that's no problem. I'd avoid staying anywhere that it was.

Your dog should have a regular sleeping mat or rug that you can take into the room. It then will understand that it is home for the night. Dogs catch on to the routine very quickly. However, I do not leave the dog in the room unattended if I am leaving the building. I'm not worried that any damage will be done, but the dog might bark at strange noises or voices if I'm not around.

There have been a few times when it was necessary to leave a dog in a room for part of a day. In such a case, the dog should always be confined to a kennel box, and the desk should be advised. Housekeepers usually won't enter a room containing an unkenneled dog, no matter how friendly it appears. A comfortable kennel box is the safest and best place for a dog in a vehicle, so I always have one along anyway.

Occasionally, a security deposit is required, to be returned after your room is examined at checkout time. I have no problem with that.

There are just a few other simple, commonsense rules. On long trips, keep your dog on its regular rations, but feed fairly lightly. Make a few stops daily at places where the dog can stretch, sniff, and do its essentials. The first stop of the day should not be far down the road, even if you've already walked the dog before loading up. Always offer water. And of course you know better than to leave your dog in a poorly ventilated vehicle on a hot day. If I can't find a shady place where I can keep an eye on the truck while eating lunch, I'll just get a sandwich at a drive-through.

Finally, you should know that, no matter how heedful you may be of the foregoing advice, you may some day meet a certain motelkeeper, or one like him, who will greet your warm smile and your dog's wagging tail with a snarl.

He was a big guy, and his motel office had an unfriendly look from the moment I entered and rang the bell on the counter. You know the type. Signs on the wall saying "This Place Is Owned By A Mean S.O.B. With A Double-Barreled Shotgun," and "We've Got Your License Number. Take Our Towels And Meet Our State Patrol."

But I was tired, so I asked about a room for the night.

"Yeah, I got one, but not for you!"

"How's that?"

"I see ya got a big dog out there in the truck," he said with a scowl.

"Yes, I have. But if that's a problem, he can stay in the truck. It's a warm enough night, and we're both tired," I answered, still trying to be friendly.

"The hell he'll stay in the truck! As soon as it's dark you're gonna sneak that dog into the room. I told ya. I don't want no part of nobody with no dog!"

"Well, it's your motel," I said brusquely. I was already heading for the door, but the guy behind the counter wasn't through.

"No dog has ever slept in the same room with me," he called after me.

I turned to face him, and for once I was struck with the right rejoinder at that very moment, instead of ten miles down the road.

"Well mister," I said. "Dogs can be pretty particular about things like that."

The memory of the look on his face still makes me smile.

6

Guns and Gunning

Good Guns

If you're a grouse hunter, odds are that you already have some cherished opinions about what constitutes a good grouse gun, and you may already have one fitting those specifications. However, most of you might admit that you also cherish the idea of owning something better, a gun that's perfect in every respect, one that literally leaps to the shoulder, finds and follows the bird like a streaking hawk, and then unerringly surrounds the target with a cloud of shot.

Oddly enough, some of us have owned such guns, but we probably traded them off years ago, during a shooting slump that had naught to do with the gun. By and by, I am going to tell you what to do to end a shooting slump, but right now I am going to tell you the one absolute truth about guns for grouse and woodcock: Friend, just use whatever works for you.

Some of my longtime hunting companions will cringe at such heresy. They are the ones with guns with engraved sidelocks, and dogs from storied kennels. For them, to pursue grouse with a pumpgun would be tantamount to setting aside their flyfishing gear and taking trout with a canepole and worms. That may

Browning Superposed and grouse.

appear to be snobbish, and indeed, there has always been an air of elitism surrounding the "right" way to gun for grouse. However, gunners with such convictions (or should I say addictions?) actually are found at every economic level and are, almost without exception, good company in camp and in the uplands.

At the other end of the spectrum, I know of a hunter, widely reputed to be the grimmest reaper of grouse in his county, who uses a single-shot 12 gauge with its barrel chopped to the legal minimum of eighteen inches. And there's Dan Werner, one of the best grouse gunners I know, who uses a well-worn, 12 gauge Remington pumpgun equipped with a slug barrel. Its stubby, cylinder-bored tube is equipped with rifle sights, but I'm sure Dan ignores them when swinging on a grouse.

There is pleasure in owning and using fine guns, but some really ugly specimens perform prettily in the coverts. There also are certain advantages to using such guns. They are rarely lost or stolen and you can drag them through hostile cover in all kinds of weather without wincing at the inevitable bumps and scratches.

Bill Stokes is an old friend, a fellow sportsman and writer, who can wax as lyrical as anyone about grouse hunting. However, he also is a former farm boy who grew up regarding guns as tools, not *objets d'art*.

One morning I showed up at Bill's cabin for a grouse hunt in the central Wisconsin woodlands, and found him somewhat more disorganized than usual. He couldn't find his gun.

"Where did I have it last?" he mumbled. "Must have left it where I parked the day before yesterday. Laid the gun down while I cleaned the birds. Forgot to put it in the Scout."

After we'd loaded up our dogs and gear, Bill calmly drove to the spot where he'd left the woods a couple of days earlier. Sure enough, there was his gun. It was one of those pumps once sold under sundry names by virtually every mail order and hardware company. Bill frowned a bit as he picked it up. It had rained the previous day and the gun was blotched with rust. The frown became a scowl when Bill tried to work the action. The fore-end was swollen. It wouldn't budge.

Rummaging around in his vehicle, Bill found a hatchet. Then, with a couple of whacks, he trimmed away the wood that was binding against the barrel. The biggest splinter appeared to be about the size of a barrel stave.

"That'll do it," he announced, working the action with an emphatic clickety-clack. "Let's go hunting!"

I will leave you to guess who shot the most grouse that day.

I hunt mostly with side-by-sides. I like the balance, simplicity and uncluttered lines of double guns, and they offer definite advantages in heavy cover. A double with twenty-six-inch barrels is no longer, overall, than an autoloader or pump with a tube of twenty-one or twenty-two inches. Also, a double gun has fewer appendages to hang up in the brush. A repeater is apt to get caught in the gap between the barrel and magazine tube. Ventilated ribs invite snags too, so I dislike them on field guns.

I sometimes do use a pumpgun with a vent rib, though, and for the best of reasons: I can hit birds with it. I acquired a 20 gauge Browning BPS a few years ago while field testing various steel shot loads. I was still wary then about shooting steel in my double guns. I developed a liking for the little pumpgun. It is the Uplander model with a 22-inch barrel. It has a high profile vent rib that invites hang-ups in dense cover, but it fit me so well that I decided to hang onto it. I often take it on trips as a spare, and it gets some use each season.

I was ten years old when an uncle gave me a much-worn Hamilton No. 27, chambered for .22 shorts. Before that, he had allowed me to use his rifle, a .22 Buckhorn bolt action that,

The gun rack at Cassidy's cabin after a day in the coverts. The guns that did duty that day were, left to right, a Browning B-SS, a Browning Superposed Ultralight and an SKB Model 680 (all 20 gauges), and a pair of AYA No. 2 sidelocks in 28 and 20 gauge.

according to Stevens Arms Co., was just like the one Frank "Bring 'Em Back Alive" Buck had used in Africa. I can remember being scolded for dragging the buttstock of Uncle Earl's rifle on the ground. I was that small. However, I was consumed with a passion for hunting, and with the permissiveness and forbearance of my elders, which seems amazing to me now, I became a good rifle shot at an early age.

The Hamilton was the cheapest kind of gun imaginable. In 1937 they sold for about $3, but also were widely available as premiums for selling magazines or Cloverene Salve ("Good For Man or Beast"). It was a hammer gun with a break-action, opened by pushing up a little knurled knob at the breech. The barrel was a rifled bronze tube within a blued sheet metal cylinder. (You could see a seam along the barrel's underside.) The sights were sheet metal too, and, since they weren't adjustable, you had to use "Missouri windage" to hit anything. The extractor was a feeble thing that needed help from my pocket knife, and the stock was simply sawn from a narrow plank. Nonetheless, I treasured that gun and shot it as much as I could. A box of 50 Kleenbore .22 shorts cost 18 cents, but the hardware store would sell half a box of the greasy little bullets for a dime. Money was scarce then.

I hunted whenever I could, both on the old family farm near the Mississippi River in Buffalo County, and on my maternal grandparents' farm in southeast Wisconsin. I was allowed to roam the woods and bluffs alone. My sister Joyce, fifteen months younger and a real tomboy, sometimes tagged along.

I was only vaguely aware that there were game laws. It may be that the taking of my first grouse was not entirely legal. Wisconsin, like some other states, forbids the taking of game birds with a rifle. It's a good law, but it may not have been in effect in the 1930s. In any event, I'll invoke the statute of limitations and tell the story.

I was scrambling up the wooded slope of a steep Buffalo County bluff, trying to catch up with my grandfather's farm dog, Teddy, whose avocation was squirrel hunting. He never barked tree, but he was an all-white dog with a luxuriant tail that wagged like a semaphore when he'd located game. So, when I saw that tail signaling me from high on the hill, I huffed up there as fast as I could.

Teddy was circling the base of a big oak. I approached with caution. On a few previous occasions, while scanning branches for a bushy tail, a "partridge" had rocketed from a limb. It always amazed me. They seemed invisible until they moved. This time though, I heard something "purting" at the dog. Moving ahead painstakingly, I finally saw it. Lordy, it looked as big as a turkey! At the crack of the little rifle, the bird toppled from the limb and began flopping and rolling down the slope. Poor Teddy hardly knew what to do, for he wasn't supposed to chase chickens. I found the bird dead in a brushy gully below. Teddy kept his nose buried in its feathers, fairly prancing with joy, as I carried it back to the farmhouse. Teddy was my first grouse dog.

That little Hamilton rifle also killed the first woodcock I can remember. Dad was with me. My father liked to hunt, but didn't have nearly enough time for it to suit me. Hikes with him were special, for he knew a lot about the woods. However, he had been raised by practical people, and did not indulge in wasteful shooting. He rarely shot at flying birds. Neither did he waste shotgun shells on things that weighed less than the ammunition expended to get them.

We were approaching the edge of a pastured woods when Dad stopped and said, "Look at that!" I couldn't make out what he was trying to show me. Handing me his gun, a 16 gauge Eastern Arms single shot, Dad asked for my rifle. He took careful aim, fired, and then led me to a plump, brown bird lying at the edge of a spring seep, maybe twenty-five yards away. I knew immediately what it was. I had seen its picture on the cover of a sporting magazine. A woodcock!

Dad had shot it in the head. The rest of the bird was unmarred. I stroked its feathers, patterned with rich shades of brown, and thought it was about the most exotic and elegant thing I had ever seen.

Back at the farmhouse, the woodcock became quite a conversation piece. "Not much meat on those things, is there?" "Are they really good to eat?" The bird was cooked with the squirrels we got that day, and, with more curiosity than enthusiasm, everyone sampled it. To the best of my knowledge, Dad never shot another.

I was almost fourteen when I got my own shotgun. It was an Iver Johnson Champion, a 20 gauge single shot that cost me $11. It had taken a year of odd jobs to save that much, and I had to earn yet another dollar for a box of shells and a wooden cleaning rod. I've owned dozens of guns since, but none have been as beautiful to my eyes as was that little single shot with its colorful case-hardened receiver and glowing walnut stock. In truth, the wood had color and grain that could only be found on a very expensive gun today.

Although I didn't realize it then, that stock was also as crooked as a dog's hind leg. It had so much drop that I could practically rest my chin on it while looking down the barrel. As a result, the gun's kick was out of all proportion to its size. Another hindrance was the strength of the main spring. Only by mighty effort of my skinny thumb could I cock the hammer. Love conquers all, however. Pheasants were abundant, and I managed to bag some. At the same time, I was acquiring some bad shooting habits that were to plague me for years.

Our family then lived in a semi-rural part of southeastern Wisconsin that was rapidly becoming urbanized. There weren't any grouse there, and there were no more visits to the old farm after Grandpa Johnson died. There was a renter on the place, and it was too far away anyway. Tires and gasoline were rationed after we went to war in 1941. Shotgun shells became scarce too. I dropped out of high school and joined the Navy. The Navy had lots of ammunition, and I got some wingshooting experience during the next couple of years. However, it was with 20 mm and 40 mm anti-aircraft guns.

Better Guns

The Iver Johnson got more years of use after I returned home in 1946. Going to college on the GI Bill didn't leave much money for new toys. I couldn't go grouse hunting anyway. The birds were at a low point in their cycle, so the Wisconsin Conservation Commission ill-advisedly closed the seasons in 1945-47. Grouse numbers were still low when the hunt re-opened in 1948, but they rebounded dramatically the next year—just as they did in Minnesota and Michigan where they had been hunted all along.

My timing could not have been better. Grouse were nearing a near-record peak when I graduated. I found a job in an area that then had lots of birds, both ruffed grouse and sharptails, and I soon bought a 20 gauge Model 12 Winchester pumpgun with modified choke. I later had its 28-inch barrel shortened to 26 inches and fitted with a Weaver interchangeable choke. It was my first real grouse gun.

That first job was at the Clark County Press, a county seat weekly published in Neillsville, Wisconsin. The police chief, Larry Drescher, was a dedicated grouse hunter who directed me to some

A brace of woodcock with 20 gauge Ithaca SKB over and under

productive covers when the next season rolled around. A big man, Larry used a 12 gauge Model 12 with a full-choked barrel to deadly effect. His gun did chew the birds up some though.

While in Neillsville, I also learned that Milo Mabee, a local barber, was a renowned hunter of woodcock. However, he proved evasive. It was years before we finally became friends and hunting partners. Milo was a deadly shot too. His gun was a 20 gauge Fox Model B double with 26-inch barrels bored improved and modified.

As for me, I kept shopping and swapping, always looking for the right gun. I will spare you the entire list, but it included a 16 gauge Model 97 Winchester (a pumpgun with outside hammer), a 16 gauge Marlin Model 90 (an over-and-under), a 12 gauge Browning Superposed, a couple of autoloaders, sundry other pumpguns and a couple of Stevens-made doubles. Most of them served me well for a while. However, whenever I got into a slump I'd lose confidence in the gun and get an itch for something else. I wish I had some of those guns back now.

I finally found my all-time favorite grouse-getter in 1972. Ithaca had recently started marketing doubles—both side-by-sides and over-and-unders—made by SKB in Japan. They looked like good, honest guns, so I acquired one on a trade. It was the Model 100, a plain 12 gauge side-by-side with 26-inch barrels bored modified and improved cylinder. Like other early SKBs, the barrels were not only chrome-lined inside, but black-chromed outside. My new gun's walnut stock had about as much figure as a pine plank, but so what? It lacked automatic ejectors, but who needed them? I had mixed feelings about its automatic safety, but figured it could be disengaged later, if desired. I could get used to its selective single trigger too. Most importantly, the gun weighed less than seven pounds and balanced nicely in my hands. I really liked the way it mounted and pointed. I still do.

For more than two decades, that SKB has served me well. My eyes sometimes stray to prettier pieces, and I often shoot other guns, but I have never had another that I trust as much, or that has taken nearly so many birds. Certainly, my success with it has been partly due carrying it through my peak years—times when I've traveled widely and hunted 100 to 200 days annually. Much of that time too, I also was hunting with good dogs, and grouse and woodcock numbers were high. My gun has always done its part though. I can wish no more for you than that you have or will find one that suits you as well.

An AYA 20 gauge and a brace of woodcock

A 20 gauge Browning B-SS rests in a corner of the cabin after a good morning's work in the woods. One of the best side-by-sides ever marketed in the medium-price range, the B-SS is, unfortunately, no longer made.

For a long time I hankered for a 20 gauge to match my 12, and three years ago I found one at an irresistible price. It did have some scratches and dings, but the gun was basically sound and tight, the bores were bright, and it weighed only six pounds.

The 20's barrels were 28 inches long, bored full and modified. No problem. I simply set the trigger to fire the full choke barrel first. In that barrel I then used spreader loads. I then had improved cylinder and modified patterns, just as in my 12. (I have loaded and used spreaders for years, and will discuss them later.)

The 20 quickly became my gun of choice for woodcock and early season grouse, but I often felt hampered by those 28-inch tubes. After fretting about it for two seasons, I had two inches lopped off, removing all choke in the process. Tripping off to the patterning board to assess the damage, I was pleasantly surprised at the performance of even cheap, light loads of No. 8s from those straight cylinder barrels. No woodcock would escape if caught in those patterns within 15 yards or so. Premium loads with an ounce of hard shot easily extend the effective range by five yards or more, making them my choice in the second barrel. Still heavier loads— up to 1-1/4 ounce in the three-inch chambers—could be used if I felt the need. And steel shot? I'll discuss that in the section on ammunition.

If you are to do all of your hunting with one gun, a 12 is the best choice. Without doubt, it is the most versatile of gauges. However, a 20 gauge is more than adequate for most upland applications, and if you prefer the 16, that's fine too.

The 28 gauges are nice little guns and several of my friends have been quite taken with them in recent years. The 28 was fairly popular among rabbit hunters when I was a lad, but it seemed to lose its allure after the gunmakers began chambering .410 bores for three-inch shells. Skeet shooters kept the 28 alive until its revival among hunters in the 1980s. In my opinion, the 28 makes a dandy woodcock gun and is certainly adequate for early season grouse. However, even with the one-ounce loads sometimes offered, it cannot compete with a 20 gauge at ranges much beyond 25 yards. The 28's biggest plus, it seems to me, is that it is almost always made on a gun frame designed for that gauge. The result is usually a truly lightweight gun. Some 20s, on the other hand, are built on frames meant for bigger gauges.

The .410 bore is not in the same league with the 28 gauge. Not even close. Although I've seen some impressive work done on woodcock by hotshots with .410s, even the experts usually reach for something bigger when going for grouse.

AYA 28 gauge double with pair of grouse.

A Browning Superposed Ultralight and a brace of woodcock.

Obviously, the criteria for choosing a grouse or woodcock gun should be different than for selecting a gun for waterfowl or pheasants. I think that light weight is paramount. Unless you're muscled like a weight lifter, anything weighing much over seven pounds is going to be hard to keep at ready while busting through the brush for hours. The ideal gun for timberdoodling might be deemed too "whippy" for other applications, but you'll be grateful for a gun that handles quickly in close cover. And, of course, barrels should be short and chokes wide.

Some really lightweight guns are available. Among the best is the Franchi 48/AL autoloader, weighing only 5 pounds in 20 gauge and a bit over 6 pounds in 12 gauge.

Among other lightweights, Ithaca's Featherlight pumpguns have always been popular. The 20 goes about 5-3/4 pounds; the 12 about 6-1/2. There also has been an Ithaca Ultralite 20 gauge weighing only 5 pounds. Guns like my BPS Uplander and Remington's 870 Special Field are a bit heavier, but still handy and nimble at about 6 pounds in 20 gauge. The autoloading Model 1100 Special Field weighs somewhat more.

There has been a long, but ever-changing list of interesting double guns offered in recent years. I've been seeing some really nice imports from Italy and Spain, and the lightweight versions of

Browning's stack-barreled Citoris, made in Japan, are popular in regions I frequent.

My only advice is that when you find a gun that you like, stick with it. It's also a good idea to adopt certain features as standards if you own more than one gun. For example, don't switch back and forth between single and double triggers. Don't have an automatic safety on one gun and a manual safety on another. Use guns that all have their safeties in the same location, too. There is no time for fumble-fingered searches when a grouse or woodcock takes to the air.

Makings of a Wingshot

Now, before we go any further, I have to tell you this: If, taking shots as they come, you consistently connect with more than a third of the shells you fire at grouse, you can skip this section. (Maybe you can give *me* a lesson sometime.) Likewise, any beginner who is able to attend the Orvis Shooting School or the like, can pass over what follows here—perhaps returning to read it for amusement later.

I feel qualified to give advice on shotguns and wingshooting only because I think I've made virtually all of the possible mistakes. I became a fair-to-middlin' wingshot mostly by trial and error, although coaching by friends who were champion scattergunners no doubt helped.

Precision shooting with rifled arms was an earlier passion. I shot competitively and was a rifle marksmanship instructor. However, concentrating on steadiness, sight picture and trigger control doesn't help much when you're trying to intercept a rocketing grouse with a charge of fine shot. I've known very few shooters who were experts with the rifle (or handgun) and fine wingshots as well.

My interest in shotguns grew considerably faster than my proficiency with them. I suppose I could have been called an "average" shot early on, for I did well enough on ducks and pheasants. However, grouse shooting befuddled me, so I continued to do a lot of trading, looking for the magic gun. That I did shoot fair numbers of grouse during my early years was due mainly to the ample opportunities I had.

Vic Reinders demonstrates his championship form on clay birds.

Practice on clay birds helped quite a bit. However, neither a partner with a hand trap nor sessions on the trap and skeet fields can prepare one fully for those winged explosions in the alders. Sporting clays would have been more helpful, but it had not yet come to our shores when I was struggling hardest to become a good wingshot. (And now, alas—with its emphasis on special equipment and what I regard as "stunt" shooting— sporting clays has been moving away from imitation of real hunting situations.)

It actually was my old friend Homer Circle, the longtime angling editor of *Sports Afield*, who provided a breakthrough to a new level of skill. Back in the 1960s, when Homer was working for the Daisy-Heddon folks, he sent me a Daisy air rifle and about a jillion BBs. The gun had a "man-sized" stock and it had no sights.

"Just try walking around shooting at things with this, keeping both eyes open." Homer's accompanying note instructed. "You'll see the BBs in flight, and you'll soon be able to hit moving targets. I know it sounds wacky, but it really helps improve wingshooting skills."

Wacky, yes, but it sounded like fun. I began taking the BB gun along on hikes around our country acres. I practiced mounting the gun quickly and shooting at small marks—an oak leaf, a grasshopper, the head of a thistle. Soon I had acquired an uncanny accuracy. It was instinctive shooting, similar to what I'd mastered with a slingshot when I was a boy. When I switched to winged targets, the cabbage butterflies in our garden were in big trouble.

It didn't seem possible that such an exercise could markedly improve one's skills with a shotgun, but it worked for me. I shot better that autumn than I ever had before. Furthermore, the improvement persisted. Ever since, when I miss any decent shot at a grouse, I am not only dismayed but genuinely surprised. There was a time when I was stunned when I hit one!

Constant repetition with that BB gun drove home these cardinal rules: *Keep your head down on the stock. Keep both eyes open. Focus attention on the target, not the gun.* Having finally learned to point, swing and shoot without trying to sight down the barrel, I began putting more birds in the bag.

If you're a city dweller, it can be hard to find a place to roam, even with a BB gun. However, there is another exercise you can do at home that I've also found helpful. It looks a little silly, so I do it in the privacy of our basement family room. (Note that these instructions are for a right-handed shooter. If left-handed, simply substitute left for right, and vice-versa.)

First, always check first to see that the gun is unloaded. Close your eyes. Then quickly bring the gun to your shoulder, as if to shoot a flushing bird. Now open your right eye. You should be looking right down the top of the barrel or rib. In addition to the front sight, it's okay to see a little of the barrel or rib, but not much. If you're seeing a lot of barrel, your cheek is too high on the comb of the stock. Try again and again until you get it right. In twenty tries or so, you should be programmed to do it the same way each time. If it continues to be difficult, you probably have a gun fit problem. We'll deal with that a bit later.

Now, with the gun lowered, focus your attention on a point some yards away—perhaps a design on the wallpaper or a knot in the paneling. Mount the gun quickly, this time with both eyes open, as if to shoot at that mark. Now shut your left eye. You should be looking right down the rib as before, with the front bead on the mark you selected. Repeat that sequence again and again, until you've got it right. If the bead consistently appears off to one side, your left eye is probably dominant, as mine is. In extreme cases, you might consider learning to shoot from your left shoulder. However, as you mount the gun, try squinting the left eye just enough to eliminate that problem. It works for me, and, with repetition, that too becomes automatic.

Do the gun-mounting exercise frequently, and do it until you begin to tire. Do it as you are walking around the room. Vary the angles by selecting first one mark, then another and another. I also recommend that you try this exercise while wearing the heaviest clothing you are apt to wear while using that gun. It can be boring, but such practice will pay off in two ways. It will make proper gun mounting a reflex and it will develop the very muscles you need to carry a gun at ready for hours and get it into action in an instant, just as you must do when grouse hunting.

A Fitting Gun

Possibly, before getting this far, you have run into a real hang-up. The stock tends to catch at your armpit. Are you mounting the gun correctly? Your arms should extend forward as you raise the gun, then pull the stock back to your shoulder. Your cheek should be waiting to meet the comb of the stock. Exaggerate the motion until you get the feel of it. You may find that moving your left hand a bit farther back on the forend will help.

Dick checks a target. A session at the patterning board is always a good idea before going afield with a new gun or a different load.

If it still feels awkward, the stock is almost certainly too long. Gun mounting should be easy, even when wearing the bulkiest clothing you will wear while hunting. Remove the butt plate or pad and try again. Now it might feel just right, or it may be too short. Either way, you have a better idea of just what your "length of pull" (the distance from trigger to butt) should be.

I think that many shooters would do better in the coverts with stocks somewhat shorter than the standard pull of 14 inches or so. For instance, I am 6 feet tall and wear shirts with 33-inch sleeves. I prefer a 13-3/4-inch length of pull on a grouse or woodcock gun, and have had no problems shooting guns with stocks as short as 13-1/2 inches. It is much easier to shoot a gun with a stock a bit too short than with one that is too long. You'll find that even a quarter-inch or so can make a very noticeable difference.

For someone inexperienced in such matters, stock surgery is best left to a gunsmith. If the gun has a plastic or hard rubber butt plate, I like to replace it with a lightweight rubber pad. You don't need one of those thick, heavy, ventilated pads made for trap and duck guns. The ones I use are made for rifles. Some shooters don't like rubber butt pads because they say they catch and slow down their gun mounting, but that is not a problem if your stock is of proper length and you mount the gun as I described. I don't like hard butt plates because they are breakable, and because they allow a gun to skid and fall when it is stood in a corner.

One more thing about stock length: Don't be afraid to take off an eighth-inch or so more than you think you want. Try it. If you don't like it, it's easy to lengthen the stock again with a spacer or a thicker butt pad.

To be sure that your gun is shooting where you are looking, there is one more thing you need to do. Your local gun club or shooting range may have a patterning board. If not, you can make do. Even a large cardboard box, such as a refrigerator carton, will serve the purpose. Center an aiming point of some kind on the big side of the box. Then back off (twenty yards is far enough) and put the bead at that mark. Don't pull down too fine. You want to look at a bit of the rib, just as when you were practicing earlier. Take a close look after the first shot. If you're using your regular grouse or woodcock load and choke, you'll get an idea of the spread and density of pattern you can expect at that range. Don't worry too much if the pattern doesn't seem exactly centered on the target. Maybe you flinched.

Now back off to the same spot and shoot several more times at the mark. Ten shots should be plenty. The aggregate of patterns then on the target will plainly show whether the gun is shooting high, low, or to either side. Just a bit high isn't bad. Low means you'll have to cheek the stock a bit higher, or raise the comb of the stock somehow, to show you more barrel or rib when you shoot. A gun that patterns off to one side or the other, or that hits grossly high or low, requires the attention of a competent gunsmith. Barrel bending is the usual remedy.

Poking and Swinging

I am not going to try to tell you how far to lead a grouse. I couldn't. Various shooters see leads differently. It depends on how (or if) you swing the gun. On the day before these words were written, I made an exceptionally long shot that doubtless required a substantial lead. However, I wasn't aware of leading the bird even an inch.

Dan Werner had bumped into a bunch of six or seven grouse that were basking in the January sun after stuffing their crops with ironwood buds and sumac seeds. The birds were tucked into a tangle on a high point, just where we thought they might be.

I was walking the ridge, but had stopped to help my dog locate a downed bird that had dived into a tangle of slashings. Dan, coming up from below, therefore arrived at our rendezvous point ahead of me. Alerted by his shouts and shots, I turned to see a grouse power diving into the valley. With afterburners on full, it banked and skirted the edge of the field below me. It seemed too far away for my open-choked gun, but the general rule is, if you can see the bird, you shoot at it. I did, and it dropped like a stone.

Due to the steep terrain, there was no way to pace off the distance to where Brighton found that grouse. However, the flight line for that one-ounce charge of copper-plated No. 6s had to be more than forty yards. I had not consciously led the bird, but a fast swing and follow-through had provided the necessary forward allowance. That is instinctive shooting, and it comes with practice and experience. Dan shouted that he had downed two birds, so we didn't follow up on the others. It was agreed that we should "leave 'em for seed."

Memorizing leads for various distances and angles will improve your scores in clay bird games, but I'm convinced that even thinking about them can mess you up afield. For instance, there was that time some friends and I drove down to southern Illinois for an introduction to dove hunting.

Wisconsin's conservation commissioners were considering a dove season at the time, and we wanted to find out more about the sport. Our instructor was to be one Jake Kringer, a state wildlife manager stationed in Vandalia.

Our arrival was met with some curiosity by the natives. They all sounded like the folks on Grand Old Opry, and each of them had some cogent—and often conflicting—advice about how to hit doves. The one I remember best was an old gent who told me, "Just remember, son, that nary two dove flowed alike!"

We were psyched up, to say the least, as we drove to the dove fields the next day. Jake was a passenger in my station wagon and Bill Stokes and I were his intent audience.

"Now you just have to remember to lead 'em," he drawled for the hundredth time. "You have to lead 'em a lot!"

At the first stop, I was placed in a swath cut through a grain field. Bill was in another, maybe forty yards distant. Jake then took a position about seventy-five yards off in the other direction. He was toting a Model 42 Winchester. (For you youngsters who don't remember, that was a cute little .410 pumpgun, a miniature Model 12.) I was equipped with my favorite grouse gun of the moment, a 16 gauge Model 12 with a Cutts Compensator on its 25-inch barrel. I had taken a fair number of grouse and woodcock with that gun and figured that doves, flying in the wide open, surely couldn't be all that tough. I'd just have to remember to lead 'em a lot.

A dove approached. Swinging the gun, I held a couple of feet of daylight between it and the muzzle and fired. The dove waggled its wings and flew on. I led the next bird farther and missed again. The next three also escaped unscathed, although each had been led farther than the one before.

"YOU GOTTA LEAD 'EM SOME MORE!" Jake shouted. His instructions were punctuated with the pop-popping of his little pumpgun. At each pop, I saw a dove tumble.

I had missed eleven doves, hitting none, before Jake signaled that we were to leave and try another place. Bill had done no better.

"Jake, I'm not the greatest shot in the world, but I'm not *that* bad!" I insisted as we drove to the next spot. "I think I must be leading them too much."

"Nobody EVER missed a dove by shooting in front of it," Jake declared. "Lead 'em some more. Lead 'em the length of this car!"

"Jake, this car is seventeen feet long."

"Then lead 'em *SEVENTEEN* feet!" he answered sternly.

At the second stop, Jake put me in another grain field, stationed Bill in a brushy fencerow nearby, and again backed off to good shouting distance. Of course I knew better than to lead a dove by seventeen feet. Jake had just said that for emphasis, hadn't he? Some doves flew over. I shot. Bill shot. The doves flew on. Frustration had turned to total embarrassment. I had fired sixteen shells, tossed a whole pound of shot skyward, and hadn't ruffled a feather. Bill was still scoreless too.

Ready to give up in disgust, I started to walk over to talk to Bill. A dove whipped overhead as I approached him. Reflexively, I raised the gun and fired. The bird plopped down between us.

"How far did you lead it?" Bill asked, viewing the dead dove with awe.

"I don't think I led it at all!" I answered as the light dawned. I thought I could hear some chuckling between the popping of Jake's .410.

Trying to establish the proper lead on a bird that is dodging and turning is an exercise in futility. If you can see the bird long enough to actually swing the gun, try swinging through the target from behind, slapping the trigger as the muzzle overtakes the bird. The faster the bird is going, the faster you swing to catch up, and (if you follow through) the greater will be your lead. It isn't something you have time to think about. The fast swing is far from infallible, but it's the best we can do.

Never mind trying to swing the gun for those poke-and-hope shots in dense cover. There isn't time, and the cover rarely permits it anyway. At such short range, one would think that the shot would catch the bird before it could move from a well-centered pattern, but we still have our reflex time to contend with. Chances are that a snap-shot aimed directly at the bird will be a miss. "Shoot where it's going to be, not where it is!" Vic Reinders used to tell me. Good advice from a crackerjack grouse shot whose name is hung high in the Trapshooting Hall of Fame.

How far to shoot in front of the bird then becomes an educated guess, but one made quickly, subconsciously. For starters, if you must think about it, visualize your shot going to the peak of the beak of the bird. The right amount of lead for you is somewhere between there and seventeen feet.

Oh, about those doves? Bill and I did pretty well after we got the hang of it. We never did get to hunt doves in Wisconsin though. The legislature decided to designate them the "State Bird of Peace." I have since hunted them in several other states, however, as well as in South America and even Castro's Cuba. They are tricky flyers all right, but not as hard to hit as ruffed grouse. No way.

And now, I promised a while ago to say something about shooting slumps. I have never been persuaded that misery loves company, but it might help you to understand this: Every gunner I know, no matter how skilled or experienced, has suffered slump periods. I know of no case that has been terminal.

Since, by its very definition, a slump connotes that you *were* doing better before, all you need to do is analyze what you are now doing differently, right? Probably not. Major league baseball players have pitching and batting coaches to diagnose their glitches and guide them through slumps. However, having experts dissect my terrible technique doesn't do it for me. The more I think about it, the worse it gets. The thing is, I *know* what I'm supposed to do.

The trick is to retain your confidence. What works for me is to simply keep expecting every shot to connect, rather than wondering if or how I am going to miss. That's all there is to it. To get rid of a slump, shoot your way out.

The Lowdown on Loads

Selecting the right shells for one species at any particular time and place is easy. What is somewhat harder is to select loads that will cover a gamut of game. I'm not complaining, but I often hunt where there are opportunities to bag multiple species on the same day.

In Wisconsin, grouse and woodcock hunting starts about a month before the pheasant and quail seasons and about two weeks earlier than the waterfowl season. Grouse hunting continues in some areas, long after the woodcock are gone and duck hunting is closed. During periods when seasons overlap, my ammunition preferences are compromises, but if you are concerned only with shooting grouse or woodcock, or both, here is what I suggest:

Light loads of No. 8s are all you need early in the season. A 7/8-ounce load is plenty, even in an open-bored 20, until most of the leaves are down. That's when I switch to an ounce of hard shot in the 20 gauge or 1-1/8 ounce of same in the 12. Not only are grouse apt to be a bit spookier by then, but you'll be taking longer shots because you can see them farther away. When all or most of the woodcock are gone, I switch to No. 7-1/2 shot in premium loads and I begin carrying the 12 gauge more. For winter grouse hunting, I like 1-1/8-ounce loads of 6s in the 12. However, when the going is tough, I often take the 20 gauge, saving weight on both gun and shells. An ounce of 6s in a premium load, with hard, plated shot, is my choice then. I rarely resort to magnum loads for any upland shooting.

My compromises? When pheasants may be encountered, I'll go to 7-1/2s for the first shot and a premium load of No. 6s for the second. The 7-1/2s are marginal for pheasants beyond 20 yards, and patterns from 6s are a bit patchy for second shots at woodcock, but they'll do, and either is fine for grouse.

If you think you might add ducks to your mixed bag, there's another complication. If shooting at waterfowl, you can have only non-toxic shot in possession. At this writing, that means steel shot, although shot of other materials may be accepted in the future.

I sometimes can bag mallards or wood ducks while hunting in the creek bottoms and lowlands for woodcock and grouse, so I use steel shot in such places during the open season for waterfowl. However, even if you don't want to shoot ducks, a discussion of steel shot is in order here. There already are some areas where use of non-toxic shot is mandated for all scattergun hunting, and, in all likelihood, we will see more such areas in the future.

To determine how much of a handicap steel shot might be in the uplands, I used it almost exclusively for two seasons. The biggest problem I perceived, other than the added cost, was that I couldn't get as much pattern spread as I like for early season gunning.

In my 20 gauges, choked improved cylinder or straight cylinder, I have found 3/4 ounce of No. 6 steel to be very effective for grouse and woodcock. At jump-shooting ranges, I have also killed several pheasants and a few ducks very neatly with that same load. However, if I think it highly likely that I'll kick up a rooster or jump a duck, I load an ounce of No. 4s for my second shot. That magnum load of No. 4 steel has worked reliably for me on large birds out to about thirty yards, even with open chokes.

Yes, I do shoot steel in my double guns, and I'll tell you why. Early in 1971, frustrated and confused by all of the conflicting information I was getting on the subject, I set out to determine the truth about steel shot. There were horror stories about barrel damage. It was also said that steel shot got harder as it aged, so even if it wouldn't tear up your gun this season, it very well might the next.

Although no steel shot was then available to the public, I managed to procure twenty pounds of No. 4s. Through some personal contacts, I also obtained samples of the ammo used in some of the much-publicized industry tests. For the next several months, I experimented with handloads. The components then available were far from ideal for the purpose, but I eventually concocted a load that bagged crows, ducks, and one ruffed grouse that year. I suppose that was the first grouse ever taken with steel shot.

At the same time, with technical assistance from the University of Wisconsin's School of Mines and Metallurgy, as well as the gun

Chips poses with a mixed bag of pheasants and grouse. Such bags are not unusual in many areas hunted by the author, and the chance of encountering ringnecks influences his choice of ammunition.

A pair of woodcock bagged with No. 6 steel shot. Gun is a 20 gauge Browning BPS.

repair shop at Badger Shooters Supply in Owen, Wisconsin, I assembled a heap of information on the shot and its effect on guns. My findings were detailed in the 1973 issue of *Gun Digest*, which might be available from your local library. I'll discuss only the most significant points here.

Sophisticated laboratory equipment showed that shot pellets used in early industry tests were nearly as hard as the barrel from an old, cheaply-made pumpgun. The shot I was using, however, proved considerably softer than any of several shotgun barrels examined. Also, tests a year later detected no "age hardening" of the shot.

After passage of nearly 500 rounds of steel shot, the bore of the test gun, a Model 1200 Winchester, showed no marring, no dimensional changes, no damage of any kind. Nor was any malformation detected in any of the interchangeable Win-Choke tubes I used, despite that the shot was in direct contact with the bore. (The shot cups then available were not thick or tough enough to keep the pellets from wearing through the plastic as they raced through the bore.)

Steel shot ammunition available today is vastly superior to what I could assemble back then. I have little concern about it damaging my guns. However, I personally would not use it in any fine old gun—particularly one of the older doubles with rather thin barrels. I would also hesitate to use it in any very lightweight gun (again, the concern is barrel thickness) unless the manufacturer says it's okay. Beyond that, in absence of the manufacturer's assurance of a gun's suitability for steel shot, one has to proceed cautiously. I have never experienced steel shot problems with any gun. However, except for my waterfowl gun (a magnum 12 certified for steel shot) I avoid using steel pellets larger than No. 4 in chokes tighter than improved cylinder.

With product liability lawsuits proliferating, I don't blame gunmakers for trying to hedge against any possible problems we might have with steel shot. Troubles are most likely when one tries to jam large steel pellets through tight chokes. Otherwise, my feeling is that problems are unlikely with any well-built modern gun. Unless the manufacturer has said it's okay, however, you are strictly on your own.

Chokes and Spreaders

I've seen shotgun chokes, and attitudes about them, change a lot in the past half century. Full chokes were the rule when I was a youngster, and the tighter the squeeze the better. Any 12 gauge that allowed a dime to pass through its muzzle was considered to be flawed. More constriction was needed to get full choke patterns than is required now. Improvements in ammunition have resulted in denser, more even patterns with less persuasion at the muzzle.

There are several remedies for guns with fixed chokes that shoot too tightly. I have tried them all with satisfaction. You can have some of the constriction reamed out, or you can have interchangeable tubes installed. It's possible to install screw-in tubes in almost any single barrel and many doubles as well. Such installations have just about totally replaced such venerable variables as the Cutts Compensator and Poly Choke, although they work well too. Or, you can simply amputate the choke(s) with a bit of barrel chopping.

If you don't want to resort to any of those things, there is still an answer. Spreader, or "brush," loads have been around for as long as I can remember, although they probably are not stocked by your hardware store anymore. The task of scattering the shot is approached in various ways, but each of them results in ammunition that can produce improved cylinder patterns from a full choke barrel, and somewhat wider spreads from more open tubes.

Brush loads commercially made in this country years ago had shot columns divided by thin cardboard separators. In one type, the shot was loaded around an X-shaped separator. In another, the shot was layered between cardboard disks. The latter trick has also been employed by handloaders. Within limits, the more layers of shot there are, the greater the spread.

I have loaded a lot of spreader loads over the years. I formerly used the cardboard spacers, a slow process. More recently I have used Spred-R wads from Polywad, Inc. of Macon, Georgia with good success. The Spred-R is a thin plastic disk on a stem. The stem pokes down into the shot column and the shell is crimped right over the disk. With a little practice, it is easily done using standard loading equipment and components. I assemble 7/8 ounce 20 gauge and one-ounce 12 gauge loads with those wads, and use them in the modified barrels of my fixed choke guns early in the season. For those who don't reload, Polywad now offers 12 gauge shells loaded with their Spred-Rs and an ounce of No. 6, 7-1/2, 8, or 9 shot.

Scatter loads are also available from ACTIV and Orvis. The ACTIV shells employ an X-wad, similar to what once was used in Winchester-Western brush loads, and are offered with No. 7-1/2, 8 and 9 shot in 12 gauge only. The Orvis shells rely on somewhat flattened lead pellets to get the job done and are available with No. 7-1/2 or 8 shot in both 12 and 20 gauge. In years past, I have also seen some imports loaded with cubical shot.

With the range of ammunition offerings today, even a shotgun with a fixed choke can be quite versatile.

7

Odds and Ends

Maps and Backtrails

It didn't appear to be anything special. Just one more strip of alders meandering from a dirt road in northern Wisconsin. However, it looked wet enough to attract a timberdoodle or two, so we decided to give it a kick.

An exceptionally hot, dry summer had lingered well into autumn and we'd been finding few grouse and woodcock in their usual haunts. To make things tougher, a lot of foliage remained.

So it was with little expectation that we turned the eager young setter into the tangle. Following the pup's bell, we slogged through a spring seep and splashed across a trickly creek. Somewhere ahead a woodcock rose on twittering wings and flew off unseen. At least the sound was encouraging.

Then Jessie's bell stopped abruptly. A solid point at last! Guns poised, we perspired through another fifty feet of alders. A wooded knoll rose unexpectedly ahead. The setter quivered at the edge of some hazelbrush bordering the bottom of the slope.

George Cassidy stalked in, uttering a few soft words of praise to his dog. A grouse flushed, rocketing toward the oak-aspen mix that crowned the hill. George's shot caught that bird just as another catapulted into the air. It whirred away as both of us missed. Ned Vespa, off to one side, took a poke too. As the pup

With woodcock scent filling her nose, Jessie strikes a pose.

bounded after that bird, the slope erupted with still more grouse. Jessie was too rattled to play that pointing game anymore.

I suppose I could refer back to my hunting log and tell you just how many birds we flushed before we circled back to the road, but then I'd also have to tell you how many we missed. Suffice it to say that we bagged one more and saved several for the next time. And there surely would be a next time. Back at the truck we unfolded our maps, reached for our pens and made some cryptic notes.

"X marks the spot," George said with a satisfied grin.

I look at that map now and it all comes back. All that and more. The hidden hill, now known as "The Nob," is one of many X's on that old map. Scrawled with notations, it has become a very personal thing. The scribblings on some of my maps are as secret as a schoolgirl's diary. They are a record of where I have been, and therefore, in some measure I suppose, what I have become.

I guess I must be addicted to cartography. I have three large file drawers overflowing with maps of every size and description. However, I'm not about to throw any of them out. Many of them are marked with places I've been and scrawled with notes about what

I found there. Others are of places I still want to investigate sometime.

A stack of old maps is better than a photo album. Frayed, marked, torn, they stir memories. They recall the sights and sounds of alder runs and tinkling creeks and aspens rustling in the breeze. They fetch back the scents of balsam, of cedar, of sweetferns bruised by boots as you hiked down a dew-drenched trail.

Exploring for new hunting spots is something I enjoy doing, in season and out, and my still-growing collection of maps has been invaluable. A canvas case stuffed with selected maps goes along on every trip. It isn't really so much that I want to know where I'm going when I leave the road. I just want to know where I've been. Interesting discoveries are noted on the appropriate map, then and there. My memory isn't good enough to catalog every likely looking cover I've poked into over the years. Those that prove special are the ones that earn names like The Old Cabin, Mattoon's Camp, Mickey's Trail, The Nob, Ace-In-The-Hole, Trickle Creek and Beeper Hill. Each scribbled reference conjures old memories, stirs new hopes. There is magic in those maps.

Dick takes a break to study his map while Kirby waits patiently for the hunt to resume.

Here is a sampling of the variety of maps the author uses for finding and recording new coverts.

Special maps and atlases for sportsmen, available at some sports shops and book stores, are always helpful. Better though, when you really want to zero in on an area, are topographic charts from the U.S. Geological Survey. One of the offices at your county courthouse probably has an index map that will show you which quadrangles you might want to order and tell you how to do so. Libraries are good sources of map information too. Once you've learned how to read a "topo" map it's almost like making a scouting flight over an area. I prefer maps printed on the 7-1/2-minute scale (one inch equaling 2,000 feet). Each quadrangle covers about 50 square miles. Excellent maps of federal forestlands and national grasslands are also available from the U.S. Forest Service and Bureau of Land Management, respectively.

Useful materials are found in county agricultural offices too. Soil survey maps, once you've learned how to read them, will indicate where you can expect to find certain kinds of cover. Aerial photos are on file there too, with copies usually obtainable at nominal cost.

Plat books, showing ownership of all lands in a county, are valuable when access is a consideration, as it frequently is for hunters these days. A plat map tells you who to ask when you want to hunt a piece of private land, and it also shows which lands are open to the public. Not every state has plat maps, but you usually

Pennsylvanians Leonard Reeves and Nick Sisley pause to map strategy on a woodcock hunt in Michigan's Upper Peninsula.

can come up with something like them if you ask around. While hunting in southeastern Montana one year, I had trouble determining who owned land where I'd seen some sharptails and pheasants. A call at the courthouse produced a map of the school district. It provided all the information I needed.

Maps put out by Chambers of Commerce or tourism groups are useful too. They'll show such things as public forestlands, hunter walking trails and snowmobile trails, any of which are worth a look. But by now you've got the idea. Real hunting map junkies can sniff out all kinds of possibilities. No matter how detailed a map may be though, it's what you add to it that gives it special value.

I suppose the day is approaching when maps like mine will have only archival value. Tomorrow's hunter might not even carry a compass. Pocket-sized devices have already practically rendered my lapel compass as obsolete as a Stone Age artifact. Using the Ground Positioning System (GPS) it now is possible to punch in the coordinates to the Birch Knoll covert, then just follow the arrows.

Ed Erickson uses a stick to illustrate a hunting plan to Nick Sisley before entering another Upper Michigan covert.

I think I'll stick with what I've got though. I want to watch my dog quartering up ahead, her every movement registering the joy of the moment. I want to see the reflections of autumn's embers sizzling on the surface of a beaver pond on a misty morning. I want to remember how the edge of that popple patch is jeweled with pearls of dogwood and rubies of holly. I don't want to miss even one minute of that while peering at yet another video display.

Garb and Gear

I'm pretty much a traditionalist when it comes to outdoors clothing and equipment. However, recalling the offerings in those four-pound Sears & Roebuck catalogs I yearned through as a youngster, I have to admit that a much better selection of garb and gear is available today. Here are my field-tested, and time-tested, preferences:

UNDERWEAR—To assemble the right outfit for upland hunting you should work from the inside out and from bottom to top. The first is easy. If it is cold enough to call for long underwear, I prefer two-piece suits of soft, lightweight polyester. The material is comfortable and durable, doesn't scratch like wool and doesn't get clammy like cotton. If it gets too warm during the day, I just peel off the top and stuff it in a pocket.

BOOTS—Picking proper boots is at least as important as selecting the right gun, and the choices can be even more mind-boggling. No single type of footwear will be suitable for all conditions, of course, so you'll probably accumulate an assortment of boots, just as I have. Including hip boots (which I use to reach some isolated popple islands in wet marshes), I now count a dozen pairs in my boot rack. Of that array, only a couple of pairs of specialized mountain boots were not used within the past year. Three other pairs are used only for ice fishing or on deer stands, so I have six pairs used mainly for bird hunting. And that's none too many.

There are two pairs of L.L. Bean's rubber-bottomed pacs. One pair is a full size larger than the other, to accommodate a pair of extra-heavy socks in cold weather. I have lost count of how many pairs of those Bean's boots I have had over the years. The leather uppers of both present pairs have been recently fitted with new rubber bottoms—a service the old mail order firm still offers for a

Snowshoes often come in handy for winter hunts in the northern states. Lightweight, high-tech webs like these Sherpas are ideal for hunting the flatlands. However, the author prefers a traditional style with upturned toes for navigating hilly country.

fraction of the cost of new boots. The pacs are lightweight and they keep my feet dry when walking dew-soaked trails or tripping through alder tangles. I also use them for snowshoeing. Their major drawback is that the traditional chain-link tread does not provide enough traction for hunting in steep terrain.

There are three pairs of all-leather boots, all of eight-inch height. One pair is custom-made (an extravagance any upland hunter ought to indulge in at least once) with double-vamp moccasin construction and cord soles. They are heavier than the Bean boots, but they do afford more support and traction when the going is steep. Well-greased, they usually keep my feet dry too. The second pair has a softer rubber sole with a lug tread. It also has a Gore-Tex liner that has surprised me by not leaking during six seasons of fairly frequent use. The third pair is of stout, fairly heavy construction with hard Vibram lug soles. They usually are my choice when a lot of climbing must be done. Those hard lug soles lose their bite after the ground is frozen, but I remedy that by screwing a few small, hex-head sheet metal screws into each sole and heel. I just have to remember not to walk across the kitchen floor with those hobnails installed, and to remove them at the end of the season. One more bit of advice about traction: Never buy boots without heels. They act like skis when you're headed downhill.

Rubber-bottomed pacs and nylon-faced pants are good choices for hunting grouse and woodcock, especially in lowland covers. The fringed cuffs quickly come with the territory.

Finally, I find frequent use for a pair of slip-on, calf-high rubber boots—the kind often found where farm supplies are sold. I insist on those made of rubber, not molded plastic. Properly fitted, and with a felt insole inserted, I find them comfortable enough to wear all day, and I often do. I wear out at least one pair per year, with the tops giving out long before the soles.

I usually change boots daily. Both they and your feet will last longer that way. And finally, while boots should never be a sloppy fit, they should always be bought large enough to accommodate at least one pair of cushiony socks. Your feet actually get a bit bigger during a day's hiking, and a change to lighter socks at midday can add much to your comfort.

Having said all that, I also feel compelled to mention that one of the best grouse hunters I know simply pulls a pair of four-buckle rubber overshoes over his walking shoes. He gets along fine. To each his own.

PANTS—Brush pants with nylon or canvas facing make lots of sense. Buy them with a two-inch larger waist size and two-inch shorter inseam than you normally wear. You want pants just long enough to keep the top of your boots covered when you are stepping

George and Jessie pause to talk things over before continuing a soggy hike in a wet woods. Those calf-high rubber boots are ideal for such travel. George is also outfitted for the task with a lightweight vest, a woolen shirt and a polypro undershirt that can be shed if it gets too warm.

Author with a grouse flushed from the conifers. He has a lightweight down vest and a soft flannel shirt under his blaze orange vest. Note too, the lapel compass on his vest and the flush-counter on his whistle lanyard.

high through the cover. They should never be tucked into your boots. The color should be brown or green, not tan (see my comments on jackets for the reason). Well-made hunting pants have durably-sewn seams and should have strongly-attached suspender buttons on the waistband.

Another clue to quality: Look for deep pockets of sturdy material. Flaps and buttons on the hip pockets are nice too. Zippered legs? They are a convenience at first, but usually a source of trouble later. Some hunters prefer to simply pull a pair of nylon or canvas chaps over their jeans when heading into rough cover. They work too. Some will even help keep you dry when the cover is wet.

SHIRTS—If it's to be the only layer worn over my undershirt, I'll opt for a light canvas or tough twill material. Bright colors are smart and blaze orange is never a mistake. I buy them a bit big because, when adding layers, I like a soft woolen shirt under the tougher one. That will usually suffice unless it's below freezing and windy. Grouse hunting really keeps one warm. However, if I need still another layer under my hunting vest or coat, I add a very lightweight down vest. More often than not, it is riding in my game pocket before the hunt is an hour old, but I do use it a lot.

VESTS—I usually prefer a vest to a hunting jacket. A vest is lighter and far more versatile. Strap vests are the simplest of all, but I like the additional pockets available in a regular vest. I especially like front-loading game pockets.

For coolness early in the season, I prefer a vest that has a nylon mesh back, even though it snags sometimes in dense cover. Shell loops are optional. I lose shells from elastic loops after they've lost their snap, so I just carry my ammo in flap-covered side pockets in the vest. Vests for grouse and woodcock hunting always ought to be blaze orange.

The author's early-season outfit includes a lightweight mesh vest over a warm shirt to ward off the early morning chill. Note the lapel compass.

JACKET—A proper upland hunting jacket should be lightweight, unlined, and roomy enough to allow ample layering for any kind of weather. The material should be reasonably water repellent and the game bag ought to be bloodproof. (Very few are, or remain so for long.) For safety's sake, the jacket should be at least partially blaze orange. The basic color can be brown or green. Lighter hues look nice in the catalog, but after a few hunts they begin to look as unsightly as a butcher's apron. Hunters should wear things that don't highlight bloodstains.

HEADGEAR—Blaze orange for sure. I want anyone who is hunting with me to wear at least a blaze orange cap. I keep a couple of spares handy for that purpose. You need caps of different weights, and at least one with earflaps if you are going to hunt late in the season. Inexpensive, adjustable-size baseball style caps are fine until it gets cold. The underside of the visor should be green. If it isn't, you can color it with a felt-tipped permanent marker. (Black over blaze orange equals brown.) Hang it someplace to air out for a couple of weeks before wearing it though. The solvents in those marking pens smell pretty strong.

If there is a button at the top center of the cap, you can remove it. It isn't holding anything together, and is just one more thing that can catch in the brush and snatch your cap off. I'm reminded, however, that my friend Harry Croy often wears a stocking cap in the brush. He says that when you can't keep your cap on, you're moving too fast.

GLOVES—I always try to wear gloves when hunting prickly cover, but I have a hard time keeping them on when it's warm. As a result, I suffer a lot of scratches and I lose a lot of gloves. By buying them three pairs at a time, I usually can find a right and a left when the temperature drops to where I really need them. Buckskin is by far the best leather for gunning gloves. It is supple and tough and it always dries soft, no matter how many times it is soaked. I use unlined gloves as long as weather permits, then switch to thinly-insulated versions that still provide a good feel of the gun's safety and trigger.

OTHER GEAR—I have lapel compasses pinned to every hunting vest and jacket I own. That way I don't have to bother changing them and I never forget them. Since I sometimes hunt in big, roadless areas, I always carry a backup compass too. It will reassure me that my lapel compass is right when I'm really mixed up. My whistle lanyard is equipped with a couple of "flush counters," which can be found anywhere knitting supplies are sold. The ladies put them on their knitting needles to keep track of the stitches. Hunters find them handy for keeping tab of how many grouse and woodcock have been flushed.

Of course, you should have a good knife and some matches. A bandanna and an extra bootlace will also find many uses. If you are hunting in dry country, don't forget a bottle of water for your dog. And even if you don't wear glasses regularly, do so when hunting. Shooting glasses with yellow lenses are a good choice.

I mentioned suspender buttons earlier because I think that suspenders are one of mankind's better inventions, but I don't like the clip-on kind. Just try suspenders and see how much they seem to free your movements. Any other gear or gadgetry is up to you. Just try to keep it simple, light, and fun.

Road Hunting and Other Sins

Someday somebody may write a book on the art of road hunting. It ought be a good seller because road hunting certainly has a lot of practitioners. The dust rarely settles on the back roads of some areas during the first week or two of the season, especially in a year when there are lots of young, dumb grouse standing along the roadsides. You really have to marvel at how fast some of those guys can get a gun into play. Wyatt Earp would have paled at the sight.

Road hunting is not hunting, of course, it is shooting, and even where it is legal, it cannot be called a sport. I do have a couple of friends who hunt from vehicles, but they have permits to do so. They are real hunters who are handicapped and who would give anything to be able to hike into the brush the way the rest of us can.

From a biological standpoint, road hunting probably has no effect. Most young grouse are destined to die one way or another anyway, and as my friend Vic Reinders documented years ago, the kills along the roadsides have no noticeable impact on flush rates deeper in the woods. Most grouse are killed within three hundred feet of roads and trails. Those that live more than one thousand feet from easy hunter access are rarely taken by guns.

Some road hunters, upon seeing gunners entering or emerging from the woods, will stop and ask how the hunting is going. I'm always friendly, and ask in turn how many mpg's they're getting with their vehicle. If they look puzzled, I explain that it means miles per grouse.

I'll admit that there is one kind of road hunting that I sometimes indulge in. We'll be rolling along on a forest road, maybe still trying to decide which place to try next, when a grouse steps into the road up ahead, like it's going to thumb for a ride. Peggy Hays, one of the most dedicated grouse hunters I know, calls such an appearance "an omen."

Obviously, we are looking at something that needs checking out. Neither are we averse to shooting that particular bird. However, we will not swat it on the ground. We will walk it up instead. Maybe.

We might try stopping seventy-five yards or more before reaching the bird, but that is risky. It might duck back into the woods while you're unloading dogs and loading guns—which is what we want it to do. However, it also is apt to take wing. The bird is much more likely to simply step back into cover if we drive by it without slowing down. Then we'll stop seventy-five yards beyond, assemble our forces, and keep dogs at heel until we're near the spot.

Odds are that the grouse has not hiked far back into the brush, so we'll be ready for a point or a flush soon after stepping from the road. Chances are also that we will flush additional birds nearby. We'll follow up those that escape, and see where they lead to. I can recall some fine coverts I've found that way.

Ground-swatting a grouse is not only unsporting, it can be dangerous. Taking any low shots in heavy cover can put a hunting partner or dog at risk. But what about shooting grouse perched in trees? I'm sure not all will agree, but I think the jury is still out on that one.

The opportunity doesn't occur nearly as often as it did in the old days, but there still are times when we spy a grouse on a perch. Usually it will be because we saw or heard the bird alight there. Occasionally, one will even start "purting" nervously at you or the dog, although more often, once settled on a limb, the bird will literally transform itself into part of the tree.

Grouse already perched in trees are tough to see. Perhaps they've been up there budding and just "froze" when they heard you coming. It happens quite often late in the season. The dog acts confused. There are birds around somewhere, but the scent is drifting around aimlessly. If you can "read" your dog, you'll start looking up. Maybe you'll get lucky and see a grouse.

Regardless of how it came about, you are now looking at the bird. It knows that you are looking at it, but is still trying to decide what to do next. You may be indecisive too. You know how hard a grouse is to hit when it swoops out of a tree. You also may be remembering that your wife has told you that she has invited two couples for a grouse dinner, and that there are only four birds in the freezer. You really need another to fill the platter properly.

"Shoo!" The grouse stares at you. So does your dog.

Now what? You've given the bird its chance. A dim-witted bird like that is doomed to soon be caught by a hawk, isn't it? Such a dumb grouse probably should be removed from the gene pool anyway.

"BLAM!" Dead grouse. But it really wasn't any fun.

One of my hunting partners unabashedly calls that "Shooting them in the pre-flight position." Most grouse hunters I know do it at times. Not all of them admit it.

On the other hand, I've heard that there are some grouse hunters who will never even take a shot unless the bird has been properly flushed from a solid point. I guess I'm still working up to that.

Game Care and Cookery

Grouse and woodcock are truly fare fit for royalty and should be treated as such, from the moment they're picked up to the time they arrive at the table. First, let's deal quickly with the matter of quickly dispatching a bird that comes to hand still alive. I have seen several means employed, including piercing the brain with a ten-penny nail. Most of the gunners I know wring the bird's neck. That is as good a way as any if you don't overdo it. It's easy to twist the head right off. I usually rap the back of the bird's head sharply on the comb of my gunstock, using a quick snap of the wrist. It is as quick and humane as any way I know.

There are even more opinions on what to do next. Some advocate using a "gut hook," which is thrust up the bird's anus, then twisted and withdrawn to remove the entrails. There are some folding knives that feature gut hooks, but you can make one by bending a hook on the end of a piece of wire coat hanger. Others like to go farther, making an incision at the rear of the breastbone and removing all the innards. The rationale for those and other field operations is that the meat may be tainted if the bird is not promptly disemboweled. However, I don't buy that.

True, if a bird is lugged around for hours in a game bag—or worse, left to stew in a vehicle for any length of time in hot weather, it might be overripe by the time you get it home. In all of my years of hunting, however, I have had birds start to spoil on me only once. They were sharptails bagged in scorching weather on the North Dakota prairies. They *were* field dressed within a couple of hours of being shot and placed in a cooler for the trip home, but they looked a little green when they got there.

Under ordinary circumstances, I feel no need to stop to clean birds in the middle of a hunt. I usually hunt no more than two or three hours in the morning before taking a break. I take care of the birds then. Same thing in the afternoon. That's also when I usually check the crop contents of grouse. If I'm anxious to know, I'll do it as soon as the bird is in hand.

The crop is a membranous bag just below the bird's throat. You can't feel it under the feathers when it is empty or nearly so, but when full it makes quite a bulge. It can hold about three ounces of food. The grouse uses it for storage, then sends the food down the line to be ground up and digested while it rests or roosts in a secure cover.

I always carry birds in the game pocket of a vest or jacket. Some like to use belt carriers that dangle the birds from your waist. Birds cool faster that way, but I don't see how I could avoid losing them while pushing through the thickets.

If the birds are not to be eaten within two or three days, I freeze them as soon as possible. It is best to freeze them in water. They will stay fresh for months that way. We usually use plastic cottage cheese containers for that purpose.

I always skin the birds. If they are to be prepared whole, I just remove the head, wings and lower legs. More often, after skinning, I fillet the breast from each side of the breastbone. I also save the thighs and upper legs, even on woodcock. A grouse's legs are fairly dark meat, compared to the breast. On woodcock the opposite is true.

We may freeze up a bunch of legs separately and simply have them pan-fried sometime for lunch. A friend who is a gourmet cook calls a timberdoodle's underpinnings "drummies" and he does some exotic things with them.

Since this is not a cookbook, I am going to refrain from describing preparations at great length. Virtually every recipe book contains instructions for cooking grouse and woodcock and

Toting birds on a belt strap (as this sharptail is being carried) is fine for prairie hunting. However, dangling a bird from one's belt won't work in tangled covers where ruffed grouse and woodcock are often found.

most are probably worth trying. Some epicurean recipes for woodcock are a little far out for my tastes though. Aldo Leopold roasted his woodcock whole, with intestines intact. I like my birds prepared with the outsides off and the insides out.

Mostly, I favor keeping cookery simple. I savor the distinctive flavor of each kind of game and don't want it overwhelmed with other things. I do like woodcock as is. Some people do not. They often are said to taste like liver. I say it's more like wild duck. However, since I like both liver and wild duck, it doesn't matter.

A woodcock feast I especially remember was at Art Schroeder's house. A former Wisconsin game warden, Art has moved to Montana, but we were frequent hunting partners for years. Following one of our hunts with Milo Mabee, we pooled our birds and turned them over to Art's wife, Meg, to work her magic on them. They came sizzling from the oven, each stuffed like a tiny turkey and surrounded with heaps of wild rice covered with a sour cream gravy. Oh my, they were good!

So were the woodcock Nick Sisley prepared in Ed Erickson's cabin after a day of timberdoodling in Michigan's Upper Peninsula. Nick simply took the breast fillets, cut them into chunks, and simmered them in red wine. Served with spaghetti in a savory tomato sauce, they were superb.

At Dick Matthisen's "Grouse House" we sometimes keep things even simpler. I cut woodcock breast fillets into bite-size pieces while Dick fetches the fondue pot and heats up 2-1/2 cups of chicken or beef bùllion. Then we just sit around the table, spear woodcock chunks with our forks, and simmer them in the pot until done to individual taste. Try three minutes. The hot morsel is then dipped into a horseradish sauce or sweet, tart mustard and eaten with crackers. Fantastic! Woodcock flesh is very filling, but I can easily put away two or more birds like that. You can first marinate the meat in a hearty burgundy, but it isn't necessary. I'd rather save the wine for the meal instead.

I'll share one more timberdoodle treat with you when I get to the *pièce de résistance* of this piece, but first, here are a few easy ways to prepare grouse.

Since sharptails and prairie chickens have darker flesh than ruffed grouse, I like them best barbecued. After skinning, fillet out the breasts and save the legs and thighs. Soak for three hours or more in a mild vinegar solution. Drain and pat dry. Then salt and brown well in a medium hot skillet with a generous amount of butter (a quarter-pound per four birds). Place in a roasting dish with bottom covered with 1/4-inch of water. Add enough chili sauce to the remaining butter to thinly cover the bottom of the skillet. Mix well. Then coat pieces lightly with the buttered sauce and place in the oven in a covered dish. About an hour at 350 degrees should do it. (The same recipe works well for two snowshoe hares.) Serves four.

Everyone loves to eat ruffed grouse. You don't want to overpower their delicate flavor, so try this: Clean and skin the bird, but leave whole. Rinse thoroughly, drain, and then give the body cavity a generous sprinkling of pepper and a couple of shakes of salt. Next, a large dollop of butter or margarine goes into the bird. An eighth of a pound is not too much. Then wrap snugly in a couple of layers of aluminum foil, taking care that there are no punctures. About 30 minutes in a 500-degree oven should cook it to perfection. The bird emerges steaming from the foil wrapper, swimming in a rich gravy that I like to sop up with bread. That's real camp food, but nothing finer ever came from the kitchen of a castle.

My wife Lorraine has another method that is simple enough for camp cookery, but also gets raves when she serves it to guests, along with all the trimmings. The breast fillets from four grouse will suffice for entertaining six at home, but figure one bird per person in camp.

Grouse breast fillets are easily parted into one large and one small piece from each side of the breastbone. Slice each large piece in two, lengthwise, so you have six pieces from each grouse. Select a pan large enough to accommodate the fillets without overlapping. (An enameled broiling pan, without the rack, works well.) Lightly coat the bottom of the pan with butter or margarine.

Now, with your oven heated to 350 degrees, dip each piece of grouse into milk, and then into finely crushed dry bread crumbs. (Ready-to-use crumbs are sold by grocery stores if you don't want to bother preparing your own.) Place the pieces in the pan, salt lightly, and drizzle a bit of melted butter or margarine over them. Then cover with foil and bake for 25 to 30 minutes. Remove the foil and keep the pan in the oven a bit longer, but don't overbake. You just want the crumbs to begin browning. You couldn't make anything any better with a list of ingredients a mile long!

Sometimes we do get a little fancier though, even in camp. This is Ned Vespa's recipe. At least, he is the one who always does the honors at George Cassidy's cabin.

George and Ned are both photographers with whom I worked during my years with The Milwaukee Sentinel. Ned is married to

Carol DeMasters, who was the paper's food editor before departing to make a bigger name for herself in the culinary field. It is suspected that Carol has had something to do with Ned's talents at the camp cookstove. Nonetheless here is how he prepares "Ruffed Grouse in Tarragon Sauce." The amounts mentioned will suffice for three grouse.

This first part is optional, but highly recommended. Take breast fillets of six woodcock and cut into small bite-size pieces. Cover the bottom of a large iron skillet with strips of lean, smoked bacon and fry until brown and crisp. Remove bacon and place on paper toweling to blot grease. Add woodcock pieces and fry in the bacon grease until they are a deep brown outside and pale pink inside. It doesn't take long! Then remove from grease, place briefly on toweling, then transfer to a platter. Crumble the bacon over the woodcock and your appetizers are ready to serve.

Meanwhile, you have covered grouse breast fillets with seasoned flour (1/2 cup flour and 1/2 teaspoon each of pepper and salt) and melted 3 teaspoons of butter to 1-1/2 teaspoons of cooking oil in a hot skillet. Sauté the grouse fillets 2 to 3 minutes on each side. They're done when they feel firm to a fork.

Remove the grouse and deglaze the skillet by adding 1/2 ounce of white vermouth, brandy or rum. Scrape all browned material from the bottom of the skillet and mix in 3/4 cup of heavy cream. Crumble dried tarragon into the sauce to taste (a teaspoon is ample for me) and then place the fillets back into the skillet to reheat. Simmer briefly and serve. Ah, the aroma!

The wine has been uncorked and the woodcock appetizers are fast disappearing (with those present using forks, toothpicks or fingers, depending upon the degree of formality of the occasion). Upon their arrival at the table, the grouse vanish even more rapidly.

Sometimes Harry and Shirley Croy are guests at this annual ritual, and Harry, another accomplished cook, might bring a fresh-baked chocolate cake. Then we'll sip fresh-brewed coffee as we watch a flickering fire in the woodstove and recount adventures of the day.

Grouse camps, like grouse hunts, are something truly special. Nowhere, not even when dining in elegant halls featuring Old World cuisine, have I enjoyed more memorable meals.

Season's End

January 31, 1995—The sun is peeking bleakly through thin, gray clouds as I start to follow the dog up the trail. The dry, grainy snow whispers as I walk. There is only about five inches of it. No need for snowshoes. It has been an easy winter so far.

My destination is more than a mile from where I've left the truck, but there is no hurry. I have all afternoon to make this last loop through the Chippewa River bottoms and I intend to make the most of it. The end of this day will be the end of the season.

The days have passed quickly since mid-September. The first month was wet and buggy, but, while slogging around in a dozen northern Wisconsin counties, Brighton and I found encouraging numbers of grouse.

Warm weather continued after we got home, keeping the yellowjackets awake when they should have been hibernating. Lack of sleep didn't improve their dispositions any. Twice, the dog and I stirred up nests of those ornery hornets, and we exited the coverts a lot faster than we entered. And mosquitoes? Some had bills as big as a woodcock's. They stayed around almost as long as the timberdoodles did, too. With the weather staying warm, woodcock offered good hunting until November 12. Then I started concentrating on grouse again.

Taking time out for deer season, I saw several grouse in my old northwoods haunts. It was another sign that the birds were making a comeback from their record 1993 low. One was flushed not far from the Mattoon's Camp clearing, where that old drummer used to hang out years ago. We never did bag that crafty bird.

Now, hold up a minute. Brighton is getting birdy. We flushed a grouse near here a couple of times last fall, but I never got a shot. His drumming log is just ahead. Ha! Look at that! No grouse here. Not even a track. She's pointing at the log. Sometimes dogs hunt memories too.

Brighton is getting sort of gray around the muzzle, but then, so am I. Calculating her age in dog time, we'll both be seventy in a couple of years. However, bird hunting keeps us in good shape, so I'm counting on us both being around when the grouse population peaks again.

Grouse hunters get pretty philosophical about the bird's ups and downs. We understand that nature's balance is really a swinging pendulum. Having now hunted through five cycles, I've concluded that the lower they go, the higher they bounce back.

Another thing: Even when the population is low, there are places where you can always find birds. Hardwood hills, for example. The steeper the hills, the less the grouse numbers go up and down.

Up ahead now is the ridge I wanted to check out. It has some cedars on top, and the far slope faces south. Unless snow is really deep, there usually is some bare ground under those cedars. The grouse spend a lot of time there when they aren't feeding. It's ideal shelter, almost like staying under a thatched roof.

Sure enough. Brighton's on point up there right now! Steady girl. Where is he? Hmmmmn. I see some turkey tracks crossing the ridge here. She's pointed turkeys a few times. It's funny to see her expression when they fly. Biggest darned grouse she ever saw! Listen. I think I heard a grouse go out way ahead of us. And damn! There goes another one!

She had that bird nailed down under the cedars. Only fifteen feet in front of her too. If I'd had my wits about me, I could have had it. As it was, I just gave it a one-gun salute. I guess I'll wind up the season the way I started it. With a miss. It really was enough just to know that they're still here though. Guess it's time to head back to the truck.

In only a couple of months I'll be able to sit here at dawn and listen to the woods awaken from winter. There'll be a drummer on that log back there, a woodcock or two will be peenting from the clearing across the creek, and turkey gobblers will be tuning up for spring.

I'll probably stop again in April to talk to those turkeys, but the drummer will be reminding me that spring is just a prelude to more important times.

My mind will wander then, as it often does, to autumn in the aspens and alders.

Dusk is nearing and a successful hunt has ended. Two hunters emerge from the woods with their dogs and begin the trek back to camp along a country road.

Appendix A

Suggested Readings

Those wanting to delve deeper into the lives and ways of ruffed grouse and woodcock will find many other sources available through bookstores, public libraries, conservation agencies and the Ruffed Grouse Society. Among those I have found especially helpful are these:

Atwater, Sally, and Judith Schnell, eds. *Ruffed Grouse*, The Wildlife Series. Stackpole Books: Harrisburg, PA, 1989.

Bump, Gardiner, et al. *The Ruffed Grouse, Life History, Propagation, Management*. New York Conservation Department, 1947.

Edminster, F. C. *The Ruffed Grouse, Its Life Story, Ecology and Management*. MacMillan Co.: New York, 1947.

Grange, Wallace B. *Wisconsin Grouse Problems*. Wisconsin Conservation Department, 1947.

Gregg, Larry. *Population Ecology of Woodcock in Wisconsin*. Wisconsin DNR, 1984.

Gullion, Gordon. *Grouse of the North Shore*. Willow Creek Press: Oshkosh, WI, 1984.

Kubisiak, John F. *Ruffed Grouse Habitat Relationships*. Wisconsin DNR, 1985.

Martin, A. C.; H. S. Zim; and A. L. Nelson. *American Wildlife & Plants*. Dover Publications: New York, 1951.

Petrides, George. *Field Guide to Trees and Shrubs*. Peterson Field Guide Series, 1972.

Rue, L. L. *The World of the Ruffed Grouse*. J. B. Lippincott: New York, 1973.

Ruffed Grouse Society, The. *Managing Northern Forests for Wildlife*. 1984.

Sheldon, William G. *The Book of the American Woodcock*. University of Massachusetts Press: Amherst, 1967.

Appendix B

Distribution of Ruffed Grouse in North America

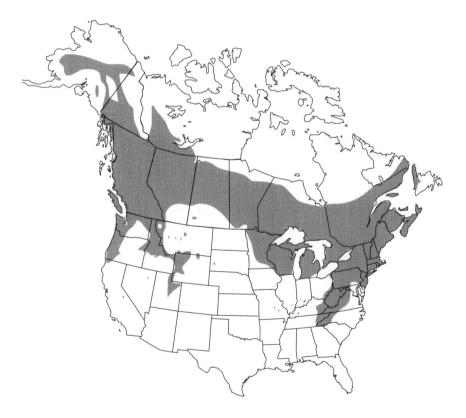

Appendix C

Ruffed Grouse Seasons in the United States and Canada

Since much research has indicated that hunter harvests have little or no overall effect on ruffed grouse populations, there has been a trend toward longer seasons in recent decades. Here are the seasons that were in effect in 1994-5 in the states and provinces of most interest to grouse hunters.

United States			
Connecticut	Oct. 15 - Jan.15	Minnesota	Sept. 17 - Dec. 30
Georgia	Oct. 15 - Feb. 28	North Carolina	Oct. 17 - Feb. 28
Indiana	Oct. 1 - Dec. 31	New Hampshire	Oct. 1 - Dec. 31
Kentucky	Nov. 22 - Feb. 28	New Jersey	Oct. 8 - Dec. 3 Dec. 12 - Feb. 20
Maine (units 1, 2) (units 3, 4)	Oct. 1 - Nov. 30 Oct. 1 - Dec. 10	New York	Oct. 1 - Feb. 28
		Ohio	Oct. 8 - Feb. 28
		Pennsylvania	Oct. 15 - Nov. 26 Dec. 26 - Jan. 28
Maryland	Oct. 5 - Jan. 31	Tennessee	Oct. 24 - Feb. 13
Massachusetts	Oct. 15 - Nov. 26	Virginia	Oct. 24 - Feb. 13
Michigan (zone 1) (zones 2, 3)	Sept. 15 - Nov. 14 Sept. 14 - Nov. 14 Dec. 1 - Jan. 1	Vermont	Sept. 24 - Dec. 31
		Wisconsin (north zone) (south zone) (east zone)	Sept. 17 - Dec. 31 Sept. 17 - Jan. 31 Oct. 15 - Dec. 7
		West Virginia	Oct. 15 - Dec. 7
Canada			
Ontario	Sept. 5 - Jan. 31	New Brunswick	Oct. 1 - Dec. 3
Quebec	Aug. 25 - Dec. 31	Nova Scotia	Sept. 5 - Dec. 31
(Adapted from *Grouse Tales*, Sept/Oct 1994)			

Index

A

ACTIV 189
aerial photos 193
Appalachians 12, 34, 39, 94
aspen buds 42, 55
aspens 34, 35, 36, 42, 47, 68, 95, 114, 115, 192, 212
auerhaun 28

B

Badger Shooters Supply 187
barrel bending 180
beeper collar 145
bell 136, 145, 147, 149, 150, 151
birch catkins 42
bird hunting 196
bittersweet 53, 67, 70
black-chromed 169
blaze orange 200
BPS Uplander 174
Brighton 59, 60, 74, 106, 108, 109, 134, 135, 136, 137, 138, 143, 146, 147, 149, 153, 154, 181
Brittany spaniel 27, 68, 96, 138
Browning B-SS 164
Browning Superposed Ultralight 164
Browning's stack-barreled Citoris 175
buckskin 202
Bureau of Land Management 193

C

canine first-aid kit 151
canvas 200
canvas chaps 200
canvas facing 198
cardboard separators 189
cartography 191
chalk marks 95
choke 180
chrome-lined 169
Circle, Homer 177
Clark County Press 167
clay target shooter 118
cord soles 197
cover 34, 35, 36, 37, 42, 47, 51, 55, 57, 58, 59, 61, 70, 76, 83, 92, 93, 94, 95, 97, 98, 99, 100, 101, 102, 103, 104, 105, 107, 108, 109, 110, 112, 117, 121

covert 6, 10, 14, 20, 36, 47, 48, 51, 53, 54, 59, 87, 89, 90, 91, 92, 95, 97, 98, 99, 100, 102, 103, 108, 109, 111, 113, 123, 135, 138, 144, 148, 152, 162, 164, 179, 193, 195, 204, 211
Croy, Harry 202
cryptic coloration 21
cubical shot 189
Cutts Compensator 182, 188

D

Daisy air rifle 177
Daisy-Heddon 177
deer stands 196
double triggers 175
double-vamp moccasin construction 197
dove hunting 181
Drescher, Larry 167
drumbeats 23, 25
drumming logs 20, 25, 26
Ducks Unlimited 36

E

English setter 131, 144
evergreens 16, 57, 64, 70, 103, 105

F

fixed chokes 188
flush 7, 22, 28, 52, 58, 59, 60, 62, 68, 74, 92, 99, 103, 104, 105, 108, 117, 121, 128, 135, 136, 142, 144, 149, 200, 202, 203, 204
flush rate 58, 121, 203
flushing dog 98, 108, 109, 133, 136, 139, 141, 142, 144
footwear 196
Fox Model B 169
Franchi 48/AL autoloader 174
front-loading game pockets 201
full chokes 188

G

German shorthair 68, 85, 104, 105, 109, 114, 118, 134, 138, 141, 153, 158
gizzards 44

gray dogwood 41, 52, 100, 107
Great Lakes 16, 34, 35, 48, 92
grouse 15, 25, 26, 27, 28, 29
grouse breast fillets 209, 210
grouse crops 37, 44, 47
grouse tracks 68
Gun Digest 187

GUNS:
.410 bores 172
1-1/8 ounce 184
1-1/8-ounce loads of 6s 184
12 gauge Browning Superposed 169
12 gauge Model 12 169
16 gauge Model 97 Winchester 169
20 gauge 172
20 gauge Browning BPS 187
20 gauge Model 12 Winchester pump-
    gun 167
25-inch barrel 182
26-inch barrel 167
28-inch barrel 167
3/4 ounce of No. 6 185
7/8 ounce 20 gauge loads 189
7/8-ounce load 184
7-1/2s 184
automatic ejectors 169
automatic safety 169
Model 100 169
Model 1100 Special Field 174
Model 1200 Winchester 187
Model 42 Winchester 182
No. 4s 185
No. 6s 184
No. 7-1/2 shot 184
No. 8s 172, 184
rubber butt pads 180
three-inch chambers 172
three-inch shells 172

gunmakers 188
gun-mounting 178
gunning gloves 202
gunsmith 179, 180
gut hook 205

H

hard shot 172
hazel catkins 42, 52, 114
hazelnut 47, 52, 53
headgear 202
heartworm 151
heat stress 151
hunting partner 8, 9, 80, 111, 112, 113,
    114, 120, 169, 204, 208

I

Irish setter 11, 56, 103, 104, 109, 138,
    140, 142, 144, 150, 157, 190
ironwood buds 181
ironwood catkins 42, 47, 55
Ithaca 168, 169
Ithaca Ultralite 20 174
Ithaca's Featherlight 174
Iver Johnson 166, 167

K

knife 203
Kringer, Jake 181

L

L.L. Bean's rubber-bottomed pacs 196
Labrador retrievers 133, 138, 139, 142
lapel compass 200, 201, 202
Leopold, Aldo 51, 208
leptospirosis 151
light loads 184
lightweight gun 172
load 180
Loyal Order of Dedicated Grouse Hunt-
    ers (LODGH) 58
lug tread 197
Lyme disease 149

M

Mabee, Milo 169
magnum loads 184
mallards 185
manual safety 175
Marlin Model 90 169
marshes 196
Michigan 14, 16, 34, 35, 72, 76, 101,
    104, 150, 167, 194, 195, 208
Minnesota 16, 32, 34, 35, 72, 167
modified choke 167
muzzle 188

N

National Trapshooting Hall of Fame
    118
Neillsville 98, 167, 169
non-toxic shot 185
nylon chaps 200
nylon facing 198

O

one-ounce 12 gauge loads 189
open-choked gun 181
Orvis 189
Orvis Shooting School 175

P

parvo virus 151
patterning board 172, 179, 180
pectinations 18
peents 81, 212
pheasant 27, 44, 79, 109, 114, 115, 117, 121, 122, 135, 141, 167, 174, 175, 184, 185, 186, 195
plat books 193
plat map 193
pointing dog 76, 99, 105, 107, 108, 109, 133, 135, 136, 138, 141, 144
poison sumac 39
Poly Choke 188
Polywad, Inc. 189
porcupines 155, 156, 157, 158
prairie chickens 72, 78, 79, 80, 208
premium loads 172
prickly ash 49, 50, 51, 100, 107
primaries (primary wing feathers) 20, 21

Q

quail 59, 94, 141, 144, 184

R

rabies 151
Reinders, Victor A. 118, 119, 122, 176, 183, 203
Remington's 870 Special Field 174
road hunting 203
rubber-bottomed pacs 198
ruffed grouse 6, 10, 11, 12, 13, 14, 16, 18, 19, 21, 22, 23, 31, 32, 34, 35, 36, 37, 40, 41, 42, 45, 49, 51, 52, 55, 65, 72, 76, 79, 84, 87, 94, 98, 115, 121, 125, 167, 183, 185, 207, 208, 209
Ruffed Grouse Society 8, 34, 36, 157

S

scouting 25, 52, 98, 100, 193
screw-in tubes 188
Sears & Roebuck 196
second barrel 172

selective single trigger 169
sharptails 72, 74, 75, 76, 77, 78, 79, 139, 153, 167, 195, 206, 207, 208
shell loops 201
shooting glasses 203
shooting slump 161, 183
shot columns 189
side-by-side 169
singing grounds 99
single barrel 188
single triggers 175
SKB 164, 168, 169
skeet 172
skunk cabbage 39
skunks 32, 155
sky dancing 83
slashings 181
snow roost 22, 68, 70, 76
snowshoes 18, 66, 68, 197, 211
soil survey maps 193
spacer 180
Spain 174
Sports Afield 177
spreader loads 172, 188
Spred-R wads 189
springers 7, 42, 54, 97, 102, 109, 110, 117, 132, 136, 138, 142, 144, 149, 157
spruce grouse 16, 72
staghorn sumac 42, 53
steel shot ammunition 187
Stevens-made doubles 169
stock length 180
Stokes, Bill 142, 162, 181
sumac seeds 181
swing 180
Szabo, Ken 8, 58

T

tail band 16, 18, 20
Texas setter 69
timberdoodle 37, 81, 83, 87, 89, 94, 95, 98, 99, 103, 105, 107, 110, 129, 190, 206, 208, 211
topographic charts 193
traction 197

U

U.S. Forest Service 193
University of Wisconsin's School of
Mines and Metallurgy 185

V

veterinarian 149, 151, 153, 155, 157
Vibram lug soles 197

W

waistband 200
walnut stock 169
waterfowl 184
Weaver 167
whistle lanyard 200, 202
Winchester-Western brush loads 189

Wisconsin Conservation Commission
167

wood ducks 185

woodcock 6, 7, 10, 12, 13, 35, 36, 37, 42,
49, 51, 54, 58, 81, 82, 83, 84,
85, 86, 87, 88, 89, 90, 91, 92,
93, 94, 95, 96, 97, 98, 99, 100,
101, 102, 103, 104, 105, 106,
107, 108, 109, 110, 115, 117,
121, 131, 135, 141, 143, 144,
153, 158, 161, 166, 168, 169,
170, 172, 175, 179, 182, 184,
187, 190, 191, 194, 198, 201,
203, 205, 206, 207, 208, 210,
212

worms 85, 87, 94, 95, 98, 100, 102, 105,
161